PRAISE FOR GUNS UNDER THE BED

"Every memoir turns on a fundamental question: How did a person like this get into a place like that? In Jody Forrester's case the question becomes distinctly fraught: How did a middle-class white girl from LA find herself a member of a deluded Maoist sect, armed to the teeth and prepared to die for the revolution? Her odyssey through the last days of the mythical 1960s touches all the sweet spots of that time even as it illuminates some of its more shadowy corners: our red-hot anger at war and racism, our alienation from the hollow promises of a corrupt establishment, and our certainty that we could heal our hurting hearts and at the same time transform the world into a place of joy and justice. But of course there are no universals—Forrester's journey is uniquely hers, and hers alone—no easy answers, and no casual causal claims. We see a young woman bursting to live, determined to find meaning in her life, and—for all of her mistakes and miscalculations—a woman with the courage to storm the heavens."

— Bill Ayers, author of *Fugitive Days: A Memoir* and co-founder of Weather Underground

"Evocative, compelling, terrifying, sad, and ultimately triumphant. A classic coming of age narrative about a woman who seeks a sense of belonging that she doesn't find in her family or her body."

— Emily Rapp Black, author of *Poster Child: A Memoir, The Still Point of the Changing World,* and *Sanctuary.*

"Don't let the *Gun* title put you off, Jody's not a strident revolutionary – she's a thoughtful vulnerable one. This is as much of a young woman's 'coming of age' story during the sex, drugs, and rock 'n' roll 1960s as it is a (former) radical activist memoir. For far too long the story of 'The Movement' has only been told in men's voices – this woman's perspective is refreshing and important."

— Pat Thomas, author of *Listen Whitey! The Sounds of Black Power 1965-75* and *Did It! Jerry Rubin: An American Revolutionary*

"Jody Forrester's memoir is at once an important eyewitness account of how American student activism in the late '60s and early '70s turned radical, and a portrait of a young woman's struggle to find her way in the world. *Guns Under the Bed* traces her journey from innocence to experience, and, in doing so, offers lessons that resonate today. Heartbreaking and edifying, this story is difficult to forget."

— Samantha Dunn, author of *Not By Accident: Reconstructing a Careless Life*

"*Guns Under the Bed: Memories of a Young Revolutionary* by Jody A. Forrester is a raw, honest memoir about a woman's path to expressing her beliefs and living her own truth. She was just a teenager in the Sixties—a flower child caught up in the anti-war movement during the Vietnam war era. A pacifist and activist, she wanted nothing more than to be heard, bring the war to an end, and live in a more peaceful society. The times were fraught with civil unrest, culture clashes, and political firestorms. From there she became a strong revolutionist, ready and willing to topple the ruling elite of the United States in the name of fairness and equality. She joined a Communist organization and became fully immersed in Mao Tse Tung's philosophy of class warfare. But how did this leap happen? And why? Can a peaceful hippie-type really transition to the opposite side of things—a side where she literally slept with two rifles under her bed?

Forrester has to delve back into her childhood to give you these answers, and she does with poetic poignancy and an honesty that will startle you. Like many adolescents, she was out to find herself, speak out, and make a change in the world. Her way. It's as if she took a journey from innocence to experience, where sometimes ideals, values, and beliefs can be tarnished by disillusionment. Her coming-of-age autobiography reveals that her internal upheaval mirrored the external upheaval around her. In light of today's civil unrest, I think it would be a good book for the YA audience as Forrester dives back into her past and puts her secrets, strife, and struggles on display in a way that is helpful and supportive. It's a lesson in finding out who you are and what you believe in, and having the courage to live it in the face of adversity. It's also about honesty and knowing when it's time to move on. *Guns Under the Bed: Memories of a Young Revolutionary* by Jody A. Forrester is a cutting-edge memoir that echoes today's troubled times."

— *Reader's Favorite*

"This memoir tells the story of a girl who loves to fight for a cause. We all know one. She's the adventurous one that we all marvel at her bravery to step out against what is wrong. She's the one who seems so sure of her beliefs and philosophy that it is easy to believe her. She's also one of those girls who is crippled by self-loathing and self-confidence issues that no one sees but herself. Jody's story is a story of that girl. It's a story of how one's strong beliefs and drive for change can get you recruited into a radical communist cell who hides guns under the bed and fights off the pigs (cops). Focusing on her life in the late 60s, Jody's story gives us an inside look into what it was like to protest Vietnam and be a part of the radical left. It is a story not often told and profoundly endearing.

    I was enamored by her story. Not just of her college life in the Revolutionary Union, but also as a child. Her hardships and treatment make you want to jump through the book and give that little girl a hug. I loved how she bared her soul to us in a way only a true writer could. Her story has many parallels to what is going on in our world today and I highly recommend this memoir to everyone. Her story is powerful and will stick with you long after you're done reading. I keep my review brief as not to spoil the story but I cannot recommend this enough. Her strength to tell her story is one that we all hope to have one day."

    — Mary Reagan Richardson

GUNS UNDER THE BED

MEMORIES OF A YOUNG REVOLUTIONARY

JODY A. FORRESTER

*With the exception of public figures,
all names in the following pages have been changed.*

Copyright © Jody A. Forrester 2020
The moral right of the author has been asserted.

All rights reserved. No part of this book may be reproduced or transmitted by any person or entity, including internet search engines or retailers, in any form or by any means, electronic or mechanical, including photocopying (except under the statutory exceptions provisions of the *Australian Copyright Act* 1968), recording, scanning or by any information storage and retrieval system without the prior written permission of the publisher, except by a reviewer who may quote brief passages in a review.

Published by Odyssey Books in 2020
www.odysseybooks.com.au

ISBN: 978-1-922311-05-4 (paperback)
ISBN: 978-1-922311-06-1 (ebook)

A catalogue record for this book is available from the National Library of Australia

For John, Emily, and Erin
Forever and Always

Revolutions and revolutionary wars are inevitable in class society. Without them it is impossible to accomplish any leap in social development and to overthrow the reactionary ruling classes, and therefore impossible for the people to win political power. Every Communist must grasp the truth: political power grows out of the barrel of a gun.

— Mao Tse Tung

Life is what happens to you while you're busy making other plans.

— John Lennon

PROLOGUE

On a morning in 2010, I went into the garage, determined to get rid of the old to make room for the new. Dozens of boxes, some unopened since our move in 1985, leaned against each other in precarious piles. Green garbage bags of our now-adult daughters' stuffed animals, board games missing pieces, drawers full of the wooden-handled tools inherited from my father—all of it could go.

I tugged first on the plastic handle of a one-wheeled suitcase with a broken zipper, but something caught. Pulling harder, a large carton lying against it tipped over. Labeled "RU stuff," it had traveled with me from San Jose to Vancouver B.C. to Los Angeles, stored always somewhere out of sight. The bent and frayed box contained over three years of my late adolescence, chronicling the only period of my history that remained unexamined in a much-examined life.

When it hit the ground, out tumbled magazines, newspapers, and documents I'd accumulated from 1969 to 1972 while a member of the communist Revolutionary Union (RU). Sitting on the paint-stained cement floor, I thumbed through proclamations and calls for political action as well as national and international newsletters from those times. Minutes from RU meetings, internal memos, leaflets for demonstrations and marches—I hadn't realized that I'd kept so much. There in the pile was a much-thumbed, underlined, and highlighted little *Red Book* with Mao Tse-Tung's many quotations of how to put theory into practice.

Two photographs fell face up on the garage floor, one taken while I sat at the Revolutionary Union information table erected daily outside the student union at San Jose State College. I'm wearing a navy blue Mao cap replete with red star, my downward gaze pensive, quiet, wary of the camera. Maybe eighteen, to me now I look impossibly young. The other picture was a Polaroid of a group of us marching on the sidewalk, me in front blowing a kazoo, holding a sign that read "ROTC MUST GO!" My middle finger pointed defiantly up. I'm wearing my favorite poncho, red with a Navajo pattern crossing the middle, a kerchief holding back my unruly hair. Again, I look so young, however old I felt at the time.

Evidence surrounded me of those years when I slept with a 30-ought-6 and a M1 rifle under my bed. So many in my generation protested the unjust war in Vietnam and marched for civil rights. How was it that I was one of only a few hundred who went on to join an organization with the most extreme of ideologies? How was it that I was so willing to put my life on the line, a life I had yet to value? Youthful conviction born of the zeitgeist of the times or something missing in myself that I sought to remedy? While it's true that much of the Baby Boomer generation felt displaced and alienated by the establishment mentality, why me?

I decided it was time to reclaim those lost years, to learn more about how I got there, and how I got from there to here. Ready finally to release the stories the box held, I loaded it back up and took it into my office to begin the work.

1
ARMED

I was home alone, a rare event in the house I shared with four comrades, including Joe, who was my bedmate but no longer my lover. Taking advantage of the solitude, I settled into a warm bath, Vonnegut's *Cat's Cradle* propped on my knees. Despite the Revolutionary Union's claim that fiction neither supported nor furthered the proletarian struggle, I couldn't give up my novels. Not even when my collective criticized me as an intellectual—not a nice thing for a dedicated Communist to be. Not even when they reminded me that in China, it was people like me who persisted in counterrevolutionary activity who were exiled to the countryside for repatriation.

Once the water cooled, I dropped the book on the floor and got out of the tub, grabbing the lavender robe with pink piping that my mother gave me when I moved six months before into the San Jose State University dorms. I wiped the mirror over the sink clear of steam, staring at my face. Still horse-like, square jawed, eyes too small and close together. I knew this obsession with my appearance was the result of bourgeois conditioning and that I should be beyond such self-denigration, but apparently I was still the same self-hating girl born, I'd always believed, into the wrong body. I tied the robe, more irritated by my mindset than the mirrored vision of myself.

The front door was open for my dog Buffy to come and go as needed. I rescued her not so long ago when she was dodging traffic in downtown San Jose and no doubt her trauma on First Street still imprinted on her feral memory. She considered it her duty to warn me when cars passed or somebody walked by. Her growl that night erupted into full-throated barks. Wrapping the robe tighter against the early summer chill, I went out to the porch to call Buffy in and saw the car that worried her. It drove slowly to the end of the block, u-turned around, continuing to the other end until turning again, returning at a leisurely pace to park across the street adjacent to the darkened schoolyard. Buffy quieted, her ears flipped back, her tail tucked. Holding fast against her efforts to herd me inside, I squinted without my glasses in the waning light. The driver was male, tall, with short hair and broad shoulders. I couldn't see his passenger, but the car itself alarmed me—a pale green Ford Galaxy, the model and color well known in San Jose to be police-issued.

That, and its stealth, worried me, making me acutely aware that I was its sole witness. Nerves firing, I telephoned Charles, my student collective chairman. He answered on the first ring. "What?"

Intimidated, afraid I was overreacting, I fought my impulse to hang up, but I couldn't take a chance that danger was not imminent.

"Hey Charles. It's Jody. Look, I don't know, maybe it's not a big deal but I'm home alone and a green Galaxy just parked across the street after cruising by four or five times." I exaggerated to cover the embarrassment that I'd likely disturbed him.

"Maybe it's nothing, but maybe you should come by and take a look, you know, just check it out."

I could hear the reluctance in his voice but, cautious by nature, he agreed. I looked out the hinged window high on the front door, relieved that the car was still there. I didn't want to have bothered Charles otherwise. A member of the Revolutionary Union for less than a year, I worried about being a good comrade and doing the right thing.

It wasn't too long before I heard his crisply chirping VW come by, its engine shuddering off. Charles came up the steps while I opened the front door. Once he was inside, I pushed the rarely used deadbolt to lock position.

Bracing myself for annoyance, I was relieved when instead he said, "Good call, comrade. Definitely pigs, I'm pretty sure that's who's in the car."

Charles made a call, speaking in a hushed whisper. He quickly hung up to make another call. I stood by to listen.

"A raid, comrade, bring everything you have." He must be talking to Lance who was in charge of our armory. "We need to mobilize, there's no time to waste! Yes, I checked with Barry and he gave approval." Barry Greenburg was the regional head of the Revolutionary Union. If he told Charles to go forward, this was serious.

Putting down the receiver he turned to me, his usual lisp more pronounced. "Jody, while I turn off the lights, you activate the phone tree. Tell everyone to wait in the alley until Lance arrives, then all come in together."

By then I was willing to take Charles's orders. It had taken me a while to give up my usual need to insist on explanations when I saw how much I could frustrate those ready to act. Being a member of a hierarchical organization, I'd learned how important it was to internalize trust in leadership.

The phone list was ranked and as a newer member, my name was near the bottom, but that night I phoned the first two people at the top. They in turn would reach out to two more and onward until everybody in our student collective was notified. Most lived nearby and would likely arrive in less than fifteen minutes.

Buffy nudged me toward the kitchen—I hadn't yet fed her dinner. That done, I walked through the laundry room to the back door. The hamper was piled high, some of the guys' unwashed shirts so funky that I was relieved to pull open the door for fresh air. Buffy gulped her dinner, then stuck to me like Velcro, sharing my unease. Outside it was fairly quiet. I could only hear the hum of the high-voltage electrical wires overhead and distant traffic until the rusted chain link gate whined open. Coming through were maybe fifteen people, most carrying guns: M1 carbines, 30-ought-6s, shotguns, Colt 45s. One woman, short and blonde, wore a double bandolier crossed in an X over an olive green army shirt with a faded nametag embroidered on the pocket. Several of the men wore single bandoliers across their chests sash-like, the ammunition pockets lined with dozens of shiny copper-nosed bullets that reflected fluorescence from the alley streetlights.

"Cute robe, Jody!" somebody said, reminding me that I still hadn't dressed. I put the kettle on for coffee and went into the bathroom to retrieve the clothes I'd left on the toilet earlier—bell-bottoms and a T-shirt with a fist stenciled on the front. I don't remember if I wore shoes.

"Jody, are Joe's guns here? We're going to need them," Lance asked.

"In our room. I'll get them."

When Joe moved in with me, I watched him wrap the two rifles in ragged towels and push them deep under the double bed we slept on. They made me uneasy but I didn't say anything, already accustomed to hold back those types of concerns that could be considered counterrevolutionary. On my knees, I pulled them out, sneezing at the piles of dust balls that sailed into the air. I handed them over to Lance, relieved to have their weight lifted.

Charles gave instructions, assigning positions. All guns to be sighted on the front door, ready to fire when the pigs came charging in. Stomach cramping, I thought I should run to the bathroom but it calmed down again.

"We don't want a bloodbath." Charles said this twice, looking particularly at two of the men we all knew to be impulsive. "They have to fire first. Those are Barry's orders."

David, tall and skinny, with his left arm shriveled from a boyhood bout with polio, was excited. Always up for a fight, he quoted Chairman Mao: "*A single spark can start a prairie fire.*"

"Maybe this is it! Maybe we'll fire the first shots in the revolution!" he said.

Nobody, including me, expressed doubt; nobody, including me, questioned our sanity. I was eighteen years old. Nobody there was much older than twenty.

Our living room was furnished from the Goodwill and Salvation Army. A faded blue tweed couch, circa 1950, stained with old food and cigarette burns, and carpeted by Buffy's black fur; two armchairs, flattened cushions draped with Indian bedspreads; a floor lamp hatted with an oversized torn silk shade. Posters were taped haphazardly on the walls of various Black Panthers—Bobby Seale, Eldridge Cleaver, Erika Huggins—as well as pictures torn from magazines of Mao Tse-Tung and other Chinese luminaries. Two silk-screened paintings from Cuba, made for International Women's Day, held a place of honor over the fireplace.

Miles, his brown hair sheared like a soldier, was placed for the first shot, ten feet from the front door. He boasted of his marksmanship achieved during a bout at military school. Charles sternly told him to wait for the command before firing, but I wasn't confident that Miles, a high schooler still living with his professor parents in Palo Alto, could contain himself. He was one of the original members of the RU, recruited by a Stanford professor. Now he was in my unlit living room, ready to kill.

Was I ready? Given my long-held pacifism that had only recently been subdued by a more revolutionary stance, I can't imagine I was, but there I stood, holding the same M1 I'd fired the first time I'd gone to target practice. Because of the myopia my old glasses no longer corrected, and my relative inexperience with shooting, Charles placed me farther back in the dining room as back-up for those in front. Pointing to the rifle, he reminded me that the safety switch was right next to the firing pin.

Lacking a table, the room was used mostly for boxes of pamphlets, past copies of the RU newspaper (*Maverick*), and a jerry-rigged long-suffering mimeograph machine. I knelt on the wooden floor pocked from ghosts of past chair and table legs and rested the barrel on the plastic seat of a kitchen stool. Buffy burrowed her head in my lap. I'd rather she stayed in my room, but knew she would only scratch and bark to get out. Some of my comrades already thought her a pain in the ass, so I always did my best to contain her when they were around.

How could I not have thought the obvious? I don't recall thinking at all. Did I want to die a martyr's death? Did I want to give my life on behalf of the working class who would no doubt think us crazy if they could see into my living room that night? I don't recall being frightened, although I must have been, nor do I think I was consciously aware of impending violence or danger. I was somebody else, the hollow me, disconnected from the drama around me, much like when I used to hide from my mother's judgments and my father's raging anger.

His face sweating, Charles peered through a gap in the front curtain. "The Ford's still there," he said. "They must be waiting for back-up." The only question was how many more the two in the car would multiply to.

Legs and fingers started to cramp. First one person and then another shifted from crouching, to kneeling, to sitting on chairs and the couch. Charles rearranged us to shifts of six up front, releasing the rest of us to buzz around in the dark. I made a pot of drip coffee and chortled at a joke one of the girls told. Tough and seasoned, she was a longtime member of the RU, and I decided to take my cues from her; apparently it was okay to laugh, to drink coffee, and eat potato chips while the guns our comrades held were still aimed toward the front door.

I went outside to sit with a boy stationed on the back steps to smoke a cigarette, relieved by the calm elicited from inhaling the tobacco. The warmth of the cement penetrated my jeans until Charles called me back to my perch. This time I rested on crossed legs, one hand on the barrel, the other near the trigger. Buffy squeezed again onto my lap, her reliance on me steadying. Small sounds amplified in the quiet—a swallowed sneeze, a muted cough, a nasal wheeze. Nervous sweat pooled under my arms and breasts.

Then.

Heavy steps on the front porch. A rattle of the door handle. Pounding on the door. More pounding.

Charles whispered, "Release safeties!" My fingers fumbled, all of a sudden too big for the task.

A voice outside yelled. "Jody! Open the goddamn door!"

"It's Joe!" I said.

"You can't be sure!" Charles said. "Ask who it is."

"Who's there?" I asked, feeling stupid—I already knew.

"Who the fuck do you think it is!" The door shook with his pounding.

I slid the bolt open. The door pushed in.

"Why'd you lock the door? You know we don't have keys. And why is it so dark?"

He switched on the hall light revealing the wide eyes and dropped jaws of my roommates to us and the guns to them.

"What the fuck?" Joe's freckled cheeks bloomed angry red.

Behind him, Craig, his shoulders wide as a hockey goalie, and Randall, short with rumpled dark brown hair, demanded an explanation. Rushing to tell them the story, we talked over each other trying to be heard.

Charles spoke the loudest. "Did you see the cops in the Galaxy across the street? We thought they'd be coming in, maybe they still will." He pushed thick black-framed glasses up his nose just to have them slide down again.

I let the rifle slip from my hands to the floor, flinching when it hit the wood. My brain skittered. I wondered if Charles knew that the bayonet on his M1 was still in striking position, if the passengers in the Ford were truly cops, what my mother wanted when she phoned me twice earlier that day.

Shaking off the hands that grabbed him, Joe walked back out to the porch. His presence reassured me, blunting the sharp sense of danger. I followed closely behind him, hoping his hand would reach back for me, but of course it didn't. Though I was unhappy about it, we were already so distant that nothing could change that.

At the bottom of the paint-peeled stairs, all of us crowding close, Joe pointed across the street. "That? You're kidding me, right?"

The Ford's windows were steamed opaque, the car rocking in the dark. Police? More likely, college students escaping their same-sex dorms to fuck.

Charles and Lance herded everybody back inside. Joe, Randall, and Craig were still asking questions, still trying to make sense of what they had walked into. Charles argued that, if nothing else, the staging was a useful exercise, a rare opportunity to examine how we might be better prepared the next time. A few of the guys laughed, snapping me back into my body and I wanted to yell, "Nothing about this is funny!"

Suddenly exhausted, I escaped to the bathroom. A brown ring circled the tub, the walls still damp from my bath. Staying close, Buffy followed me in. Did Charles say "next time"? I needed to be alone, to shake myself from the existential otherworldliness of the past two hours.

I leaned against the sink, "what ifs" spinning through my mind that I quashed as soon as they popped up. I wasn't ready to let my ties to the RU weaken, truly believing that the communist ideal of triumph over self was the best way to live given that being myself had never made me happy nor helped even a little bit to make the world a better place.

I flushed the toilet in case anyone was listening and opened the door. Buffy jumped ahead, running to hide behind the couch when the sharp cracks from single bullets being expelled from clips and magazines ejected from rifles echoed through the house. Somebody was on the telephone ordering pizza for delivery. Charles, Joe, and Randall argued and yelled, Joe appalled that we had armed ourselves to take unilateral action without back-up from the masses. David stood in the kitchen warbling the *Internationale,* the French left-wing anthem.

For decades, that night we armed ourselves in fear of the Ford parked across the street played over and over in my dreams, waking me always with paralyzing terror. Sometimes the guns were only poised; a few times they fired in a cacophony that merged with my buzzing alarm clock. Sometimes I was the one walking in the door, sometimes we turned the guns on each other, playing war games in the scrub and wind-chiseled rocks of the field we practiced in. Always, I could feel the pressure of my finger on the cold metal trigger.

Like watching a television on mute, I can still see where each person sat or stood, see the firearm they held, even what they were wearing—Lance in worn brown corduroys, Meg in hand-sewn paisley bell-bottoms, Miles in a silk-screened Che Guevara T-shirt. I remember my neck clenched tight, the weight and cold of the rifle, the warmth of Buffy on my lap. What remained opaque to me even now, more than forty years later, was what I was feeling, what I was thinking. I've tried and tried but cannot re-inhabit the person I was that summer night, or on so many other nights when I was burning with a fire stoked by an ideology that promised so much. I will never know the answer to what seemed the most important question: would I have pulled the trigger? From the perspective of adulthood, I can't conceive that I would have, but I can't rewrite that night when the collective voice trumped my own.

Only in retrospect did I realize that the risks we took were like a dropped stitch in a knitted sweater, revealing the holes only once it was finished.

2

SHAMED

My first fully scenic memory was linked to the appointment my mother made for my sister, age six, and me, age four, to see a child psychiatrist. Where in 1956 she would have gotten the idea, I can't imagine—maybe from magazines in the grocery store checkout lines or the after-school radio talk shows she favored. It certainly wasn't a decision made by anyone else I knew from that time.

Very early there might have been good times between my sister and me, playing with our dolls or card and board games, but mostly we fought—pinching, kicking, punching, and a lot of screaming. Our fistfights were legendary in the neighborhood, continuing until I was about ten, when I was big and bold enough that I could finally hurt her more than she could hurt me.

I could see how as a little sister I would have been annoying, even intrusive, being the proverbial wild second child, but my sister and I seemed born to acrimony. I often wondered how that happened when in so many other families the siblings were close despite clashes, arguments, and jealousies. What could explain, from the beginning, how deep our enmity was? Years later, I came to understand that it was my mother's doing, that she could only favor one of us at a time. If one was good, the other was bad. When, as an adult, it was my turn to be her favorite, she would tally up her disappointments and frustrations with my sister. But when we were young she preferred my older sister, who even at five could say with confidence, "Mommy loves me best!"

Our mother's call to the psychiatrist was the result of these fights. She could no longer stand living in a "war-zone," as she described it to the doctor. She needed help.

Dr. Frank didn't look anything like my mother or her friends. No lipstick. A bun atop her head like a twiggy bird's nest tightly wound and severe. In my memory, she wore all black, was solid and squat, and spoke English cadenced with an accent similar to my grandparents' Yiddish, only more pronounced.

She directed us to sit on three adult-sized chairs in front of a massive wood desk that she positioned herself behind as if enthroned. My feet stuck out in front of me. I played with the new white shoestrings on my red Keds until my mother swatted my hand. Wall-lined bookcases like the ones in the public library sagged with large leather-covered tomes. Thick curtains blocked the daylight. I remember dark, only dark.

I didn't notice Dr. Frank leaving her side of the desk until I felt her fist strike under my chin.

THWACK!

She smacked shut my slack jaw, making me bite my tongue. By reflex, I punched her, my fist sinking into her soft abdomen, making my mother and sister gasp.

"Oh, Jody, how could you?" My mother's voice was shaky.

I burst out crying. "But she hit me first!"

"Quiet now!" She flushed red and looked ready to cry herself.

"It's not fair!" Fairness, I believed then and still do, ought to matter.

Stunned, I watched Dr. Frank go to my sister and give her the same thwack under her chin.

Tears drizzled down her cheeks, but her hands remained clutched on her lap. Dr. Frank nodded to my mother and patted my sister on the head.

"She's a good girl," she said.

Now I hated them both and looked again to my mother, but she didn't look back, just kept her eyes on the doctor. Maybe she thought her jaw would be next.

The doctor's lower lip sucked in the jut of her chin. "That child must be punished," she announced, pointing to me. I squirmed, tears soaking my face and dropping on my pink-striped shorts.

"Perhaps you hurt her." My mother's usually assured voice was small, smaller than I knew possible. "Maybe she's too young to understand?"

"Nonsense. Clearly she hasn't learned to respect her elders, she doesn't know right from wrong. Children like this always end up as criminals! Did you know that?"

My ears perked. I knew about criminals. They were bad. So was I. Was I a criminal?

I flinched as Dr. Frank came near, afraid she was going to hit me again, but instead she grabbed my arm, pulling me off the chair so quickly that I couldn't rally to resist. She marched me across the hall to another room.

It took her a moment to find the light switch. Palpable darkness, her hand gripping my shoulder—the recollection can still make me shake. But when the lights came on, a dazzling fairyland was revealed. The same dark wood bookshelves lined the walls, but these were filled with toys, no two alike. On the floor were child-sized tables and chairs with tea dishes, a train set, and an unbelievable array of dolls, all magical in the fluorescent-lit dust motes floating in the room. But the most beautiful thing that I'd ever seen was a miniature carousel, just at eye level, with six horses each attached to their own painted rail. Impossibly delicate tiny saddles and bridles painted in bright reds, blues, and yellows. I didn't dare touch it, though I wanted to so badly. Still, she knew. I watched Dr. Frank pick it up and thought she was taking it away, but instead she placed it on the copper-blotched linoleum next to my feet.

"Is this what you want? You're allowed only one toy to play with and nothing else. Only one. Do you understand? Look around, there's nothing else you can choose, even touch. Only this carousel!"

Whatever I did or said must have convinced her. She let go of me and in a second was out the door, pulling it shut behind her.

The lock clicked shut. Loudly. In the very large room with no windows to the outside, I was alone. I looked up to see my mother peering through a small rectangle of glass high in the door. Turning my back to her just to show her, certain that she would come in and swoop me up. Except, seconds later, when I turned around she was no longer there.

Knees crossed, I stayed on the floor, playing again with my shoestrings, deliberately untying them. Looking sideways at the carousel, my fingers ached to touch it, but I wasn't going to do what Dr. Frank wanted, no matter what. Still, it was so hard not to. Where at four did I find the depth of anger and strength to resist such an offering?

Worse, I had to pee very badly.

After what seemed like a long time, too long, I ran to the door and pounded. By now I was weeping, choking, and screaming. "I'm sorry, I'm sorry, Mommy, please let me out, I'll be good, I promise! Mommy, please!"

Why wouldn't she come? Even at four, my life already felt precarious. My dad was always angry, my mom always busy, always ready to push me away. Being left alone in a strange place was top on my list of fears. How could my mother not realize this?

Wrenching sobs quieted to sighing tears. I curled myself into a tight ball on the floor, my hands still spread wide against the door. How much longer I was there, I have no idea, but I was nearly asleep when Dr. Frank tried to push the door open. I rolled out of the way and she reached for me, but I ducked her grasp to run out and down the stairs to the parking lot, leaving splotches of pee on each step.

The car was where we left it. I ran faster, jerked open the backseat door, and scrambled in. I didn't know my mother was right behind me. She reached in, her hand touched my face, but I kicked her off. I, who every second, every minute, every hour of my life, craved just this sort of touch pushed her away, having just discovered that she was no longer to be trusted.

The deep wellspring of humiliation and self-loathing generated that day were the earliest seeds of a self-destructive sense of shame that would become my lifelong shadow companion. I've thought a lot about those punches Dr. Frank and I exchanged and could only conclude the obvious: from an analytic point of view, the way my sister and I responded revealed our basic natures. I was rebellious, defiant, and impulsive. My sister was compliant and yielding. She was good, I was bad. It was as complicated and as simple and as devastating as that.

The negative effects of that session never fully eased. Years later, a parent myself, I asked my mother about that visit to Dr. Frank. We were in her kitchen. I was drying dishes; she was sponging the white tiled counter. This was where most of our conversations occurred, the one time and place that although she was busy she wasn't rushing around, bent on her list of what to get done that day. I wanted to know why she left me in the room and what she did while I was there alone. Instead of answering my questions, she went on a rant.

"That awful woman! She said it was my fault. That I failed to teach you right from wrong. I shouldn't have paid her—she wasn't worth even a dollar. Imagine. Blaming me!"

Dropping the soapy sponge in the sink, my mother peeled off her rubber gloves still slick with bubbles and left the kitchen. Even then, already in my thirties, I hoped she would soothe me, but I should have known better. My mother would never open her arms to me, never comfort me, never say what I needed to hear.

For years I'd had difficulty describing my mother. Something's missing, I would say, but it wasn't until I became an adult that I realized what it was—she lacked empathy. She was a cheerful person, a friend to all. Her hairdresser was often at our dinner table, as well as the woman who did her nails, but toward me there was a mysterious absence. Something key wasn't there, something that left me wondering for years how it was that she had so much love for others and so little for me. She was dutiful and responsive to my immediate needs, but I never felt safe in our home. I only began to understand once my own daughters were born and I saw how she was with her grandchildren. On the phone with her friends, she spoke of them with affection, proudly telling details of all they did and said, but her interaction with them was always from a distance. She'd put them in front of her television set rather than play with them and never hug them just for the sake of having them near.

In fact, my mother chided me for holding them as infants

other than when necessary to change or feed them. When friends of mine, with babies of their own, moaned about their sleepless nights, she would offer advice that said it all: "When Jody would wake up, I put a handful of Cheerios in her crib and she would gum them without complaint! That always bought me at least a few more hours of sleep." She looked around brightly, anticipating their acknowledgement for solving their problems.

Instead, they were sorry for me. Of course I didn't cry—I learned early that all it would get me was a bowl of Cheerios.

3

REBELLION

When I was in the third grade, I wanted to be Mexican. I added an "a" to my name, thinking Jodia sounded Spanish, and insisted my family call me that (they didn't). We lived in a lower-middle-class neighborhood on the edge of Venice in California, in a green house with windows edged by white shutters. In the playground a few blocks away, I would sit on the swing I always claimed as my own, beguiled by the multi-generations of Mexican families that every weekend made themselves at home as if in their own backyards. Grandparents, in chairs they had brought themselves, were settled under staked umbrellas. The men barbequed in the park's concrete pits while the women spread out blankets and unloaded boxes and ice-chests of food. Amid a riot of screams, the children were let loose, and I watched them with envy. The older boys lifted their younger sisters and brothers onto the jungle gym, slides, and seesaw, making sure they were okay, all the while teasing and making them laugh in ways that I had never seen white big brothers do. I imagined their lives to be an endless picnic. More than the 1950 stereotypes in *Father Knows Best* and the *Donna*

Reed television shows, these people epitomized to me the perfect family.

Across the street from the playground was a swamp that was home to many hoboes, as the homeless were called in the fifties. Warned away by our parents with threats of quicksand that could swallow a child whole, let alone the dangerous men who lived there, it was an irresistible draw for an adventurous rule-breaking child like me. I was nine the first time I ventured there with my best friend Lana. Having no idea what quicksand looked like, we stepped carefully to avoid any small puddle that might suck us in.

What was called a swamp would be known as wetlands today, but that wasn't yet understood. On that day, Lana and I came upon several men sitting around a small fire sputtering in a circle of blackened rocks. Blankets lay tangled in sloppy piles next to where they drank from tin cups. Their faces were leather-brown with dirt-grimed wrinkles. One man, almost toothless, smiled and invited us over to share a loaf of Wonder Bread, the thin slices of white almost transparent. I should have been scared but their friendliness made me instantly comfortable. Lana not so much, but she was already accustomed to my leadership so she stood nearby although a little farther away.

A grizzled old man shook out a blanket and invited us to sit. Lana pulled at my arm whispering, "No Jody, we should leave."

"That would be rude," I whispered, but not quietly enough.

"It's okay, little girl. We don't bite." Their laughter was friendly, not at all threatening. I sat down and finally Lana joined me.

"If our mothers found out we were here, they'd kill us!" she whispered into my ear.

"They won't. C'mon, just for a few minutes."

I'd always had an insatiable interest in lives different from my own. Indeed, that was why I read so much, loving the alternate possibilities and transports into other worlds.

After that day I brought the men oranges or apples and whatever I could steal from our cabinets that my mother wouldn't notice missing. Then came the tractors to clear and flatten the land for a nine-hole golf course. I asked my mother what would happen to the hoboes; whether she answered I don't recall. The beach wasn't far away. Maybe they moved there. It wasn't long before I forgot about them.

Our ranch-style house stood at the bottom of a long steep hill, perfect for racing down on roller skates and bikes. Competition between the neighborhood kids was fierce and with the exception of a boy named Jimmy, I was faster than the rest. The rapid pace, the swooping around curves with the wind lifting my ponytail, was such a high that later in life I would try to replicate the feeling with speed.

Inside the closet in my blue bedroom was a trapdoor. It opened to the underground crawl space where the furnace and water pipes lay in an ordered design. I went down mostly when I was locked in my room for punishment. Maybe I interrupted, maybe I was too loud, maybe I hit my older sister, but I spent a lot of time down there in an alternative world of my own making. This was also the place I'd go to escape my loneliness, to relieve my anger at my mother, father, or sister, and for a place far removed from their hearing to sob and feel sorry for myself. I cried a lot in those days, overwhelmed by emotions I didn't understand. I knew even then that my mother and father didn't love me. Would they have been so mean to me if they did? Their constant threat, always hovering, was that if my unacceptable behavior didn't cease I would be exiled to a home for bad children. That threat, oft made, never failed to precipitate fear and despair.

The dirt was often skin-chilling cold so I made a nest with torn towels from the rag pile. In the dark, I'd sit with a flashlight surrounded by my favorite Nancy Drew and Black Stallion books along with the plastic horses I obsessed over. Misty a pinto, Black an Arabian, Eric a high-stepping Morgan, Pinkie a Shetland pony. I played with them for hours, corralling them within the pipes closest to the ground, jumping them over the higher pipes, racing them on a track I scratched out in the dirt. All this was done on my knees—I was too tall to stand. I read the books over and over, fantasizing about my future life as a girl detective or a jockey. When I tired of all that, I had a pack of cards to play endless games of solitaire.

My parents knew nothing about my private universe beneath their house, but I knew from their footsteps where they were. I could hear their conversations and the television and radio and took great pleasure in knowing that they had no idea I was so close. Always careful to cover my tracks, I made sure to close the sliding closet door before lifting the trapdoor. When I emerged, the cover was carefully replaced and the door quietly closed again.

The day came when I was underground and my mother was across the street for her daily coffee klatch with the neighbor women. Sure that she would be gone for at least an hour, I went down into the crawlspace to play with my horses when, without warning, she came home and opened my bedroom door, calling to me to come out.

"I need to talk to you, Jody. Come into the kitchen at once." Her voice told me I was again in trouble. For a moment I vacillated, but when she called again, I didn't move, hoping she wouldn't notice the closet door I'd just that once left open.

"She's not in there," my mother said to my father, who must

have been right next to her. If so, he'd come home early from work, which didn't bode well for me.

"Of course she is! Or more likely she snuck out while you were across the street gabbing with Garnet." His voice was tight and displeased. He didn't like most people, but the women who gathered in the afternoon after they returned home from their part-time jobs were who annoyed him the most.

Their footsteps trod the thin nylon carpet as they walked into the hallway, then to the living room. Again, they called my name. Anger colored their voices, making my stomach and neck cramp. I moved deeper into the crawlspace until I was under the kitchen where I could smell chicken baking. Out on the front porch my mother asked my sister, who was playing handball against the garage door, if she had seen me. My father's heavy steps continued through the house as he called my name. A jubilant sense of freedom and the possibility of immunity from their scolding excited me. They'd never find me; I would stay down there forever, just sneaking out in the middle of the night for food and to use the bathroom. I stuck out my tongue toward their voices, giggling to hear their increasingly desperate attempts to find me.

Now they were both outside, their voices calling my name fading as they went further away. Gripped by sudden fear, I scrambled out to slide under my bed, not taking the time to replace the hatch door. Their voices came closer again, my mother's now more panicked than angry, my father reassuring her that I must be close by.

Light footsteps came into my room—it must be my sister. I could see her navy blue tennis shoes from under the turquoise quilted bedspread.

"Did you look under the bed?" She pulled up the cover and peeked into the dark. "Here she is! Mommy, Daddy, come here,

I found her!" She grabbed my leg. I kicked her off, but she held on and pulled me out.

My mother rushed over. "Didn't you hear us calling, Jody?"

I opened my mouth wide in a fake yawn. "I was sleeping, I didn't hear anything."

"Why are you covered with dirt?" My father's voice heightened to a roar. "Where were you? And don't you dare lie to us!"

I couldn't help looking over to the closet. His head turned and I knew immediately that he saw the open door. He took a few steps closer and I closed my eyes when he noticed right away that the trap door was askew.

"What did you do?"

By then I was standing. My mother drew her arm back the way she did, then propelled it forward to hit me hard across the chest. I spun, careening into my sister who pushed me to the floor. I lay there crumbled, defiantly holding back the tears that pushed against my eyelids.

My dad left the room, returning in record time with his hammer, a handful of nails and a 2x4 board. "We're ending this right now!"

"Wait," I cried out. "Misty's down there and my books!"

He was already pounding nails into the narrow board across the hatch, ignoring my pleas while my mother gathered up the horses still in my room. "You can't have any of them, Jody. Not for a month at least, depending on how you behave, and if you don't, you'll never see them again."

"I hate you!" I yelled as they slammed my door shut and turned the key to lock me in.

I heard my mother's voice—it sounded like she said "I hate you, too," but it was said too softly and I couldn't be sure.

* * *

The phone rang too early one morning. My parents' and my bedroom were close—I heard my mother groan. Her friends knew better than to call before eight on a Sunday morning. I was out of bed and crouching outside her bedroom's open door by the second ring, knowing already what was about to happen.

"Hello?" she said.

My new aunt's voice barreled through the receiver. I could hear my name.

My mother interrupted. "Wait, Ethyl, hold on a second. Are you saying my eight-year-old daughter stole your diamond ring? Why would she do that?" A scrabble of words spit again through the headset.

I badly needed to pee, but squeezed my legs tight, held my breath, and bit down on my lip hard enough to taste blood.

"Look, Ethyl, you don't know us very well so I'll excuse your inference that my daughter is a thief." My mother was now fully awake, her voice tight.

Aunt Ethyl's voice jumped up another octave. I could almost but not quite make out what she was saying. I heard my name again.

My mother interrupted, using the voice that always brought my sister and me in line. "No, she's sleeping, I'm not going to wake her just to have her tell me what I already know. Keep looking—you'll find it." She hung up the phone with a cringe-inducing bang.

"What was that about?" My father's drowsy voice was still thick with sleep. He too valued a Sunday morning lie-in.

"Ethyl can't find her engagement ring and thinks Jody stole it. Do you believe the nerve of that woman?"

I couldn't hold it any longer and stood up, turning toward the bathroom, but froze when I heard my father's voice.

"She's an idiot, we knew that. Simmer down, it's too early for histrionics."

"My poor brother—he must have paid a fortune. Who needs a diamond that big anyways?"

I think I wanted to get caught, to have this over with, but now I was stuck. Even worse than my betrayal of my mother's trust would be forcing her humiliation in front of her detested sister-in-law.

In my defense, Aunt Ethyl started it when she stole my uncle. The one who would take my sister and me to the beach in his blue pick-up truck and never scold when we dripped snow cones or left the seat sandy. I didn't hate her, not right away, not until I realized that I hadn't seen Uncle Philip since their wedding two months before. When we (my mother, father, sister, grandmother, and me) were invited to their new house for dinner, I was excited but once there, other than a hug in greeting, my uncle paid me little attention.

My mom rolled her eyes at her mother, whose eyes shushed her back when Aunt Ethyl served frozen lasagna on a picnic tablecloth set with wedding china and cut-crystal glasses. I giggled, delighted to witness their intimate exchange. A jar of spaghetti sauce, sides dripping, was put out next to the arrangement of plastic flowers on the table.

My father chided Ethyl for serving decaf instead of real coffee. He wouldn't stop grumbling about it. Her lips tightened, deepening the creases to parentheses on either side of her mouth. After dinner, during which Ethyl talked nonstop, the adults moved to the living room to drink cocktails and smoke cigarettes. My sister joined them but I shook off my flip-flops, slid them between my fingers, and bent low, swinging my arms like ice-skaters do, sliding my feet in the thick wool carpet all the way down the hall to my aunt's and uncle's bedroom. The scent of perfume, Chanel No. 5 my mother had told me, became more pungent the closer I got to their door.

Their bedroom was immense, much larger than my parents'. A peppermint pink dressing area with two poles of Aunt Ethyl's clothes hung on parallel walls. I was immediately seduced by an oversized mirror framed in lit bulbs over a marble-topped table strewn with open jars of cream and rouge. My eyes narrowed on a diamond ring that sat dead center amongst scattered red-stained cotton balls, wire curlers, and bobby pins. The stone reflected cascades of rainbows in the mirror. I reached out a finger to pick it up—I only wanted to look closer.

"Jody, where are you? It's time to go!" My mom was coming down the hall, her voice close, impatient. "Come on, your dad and sister are already in the car!"

If I hadn't seen my fist closing around the ring in the mirror, I wouldn't have believed it. Looking back, that was the night one split into two, the night when I learned there were two me's, the inside me and the outside me. That I could take the diamond ring without consciousness of the act left me dangling in some place in between self-awareness and oblivion.

I shoved the ring deep into the pocket of my pink-striped shorts before bolting. Stealing the ring would mark me, that I knew immediately, but I couldn't make myself return it.

Mom was at the bedroom door watching me wiggle my feet back into my thongs. "Get going, you're usually the first one out!"

I rushed out and was nearly at the front door when my mother called me back to say thank you and good night.

Uncle Philip bent down and lifted my chin. "Hey, it's still hot out. How about a day at the beach? We haven't made it down at all this summer."

"Yes!" I said. The ring burned in my pocket and I was about

to run back to their bedroom to dispose of it when he said, "Your Aunt Ethyl has never been, can you imagine that? We can teach her to body surf." He stood with hands now in his pockets, smiling down at me. "What do you say?"

Nothing. I had nothing to say, and could only mumble thanks before dashing to the car and climbing in the back seat on the driver's side. It was my turn to sit behind my mother but my sister was already there. Neither of us liked sitting behind our dad who swatted us when our feet touched his seat back. It didn't occur to me to argue. I just wanted to get home and disappear into sleep.

During the thirty-minute ride, my hand clutched the ring until the sharp tines broke my skin. The cutting pain felt good and I tightened my grip. In the front seat, my mother groused about the meal, made fun of Ethyl's all-blond furniture, and wondered whether she was really in love with her brother or only in love with his money. How could they not notice that I wasn't the same girl who had sat in the car on the way over? Miraculously, they didn't. In one impulsive moment I stepped outside of the invisible circle that was my family. They had to know, they must, but it wasn't until my mother tucked me into bed—I liked the covers tight—that loneliness sank in. I had gone too far. There was nobody I could confide in.

I only knew that I had to get rid of the ring, to put it somewhere it could never be found.

I waited for a long time, until all the lights were out, then slipped out of the tight covers before crawling through the living room, through the kitchen, to the side door next to the washer and dryer. It still was impossible to believe that I wouldn't get caught. Even when I was flinging the ring as far as I could into the ivy-planted slope behind our house, I was waiting for a light to come on, for my father to come outside brandishing the baseball bat he kept by the door. I didn't crawl but ran on tiptoes back to bed and fell asleep on top of the spread.

Nothing was said the next day. Aunt Ethyl's call wasn't brought up, not even when I pleaded a stomachache to stay home from school. Instead, my mother allowed me to lie on the couch with the red hot water bottle against my tummy and watch cartoon re-runs. She sat with me and laughed at the stupid antics of the roadrunner—it was all I could do to keep my mouth shut.

Crazed by thoughts that my father might find the ring when he trimmed back the ivy—how could I not have thought of that. But he didn't and I got busy and for many years, the theft hid away in one of my many mental compartments. Every so often the memory surfaced but it felt so vague that I wondered if I made the story up. I did that a lot, making up stuff. It all happened so quickly that I wasn't really sure. I often felt empty, the same emptiness that was often my default emotion when I was confused. I never told anybody, though came close once or twice. Many years later, my uncle's brain trampled by metastatic cancer, I whispered my secret to him. His hands flailed but he looked me straight in the eye and winked as if to say it doesn't matter. But maybe he didn't—maybe I just wish he had.

More than forty years later, the green house was on the market. Flags in front, I couldn't resist the open house. Looking at the ivy still there, the leaves bending toward the western sun, I found it hard to believe that a thoughtless act was now lost forever in the green burial ground. A secret buried forever.

* * *

I started shoplifting. Perhaps it was rebellion, perhaps I felt my parents to be unfair, perhaps I was sick of the days-of-the-week underwear and pajamas that I got every birthday and nothing else. The first things I stole were plastic envelopes of stamps for my burgeoning collection from a revolving stand in our grocery store. I'd asked but my mother wouldn't buy them for me. She had just started a full-time job. "Money is tight," she'd said. While she pushed the cart up one aisle then another, I was often left alone in the aisle of books where I could sit on the floor and read Archie and Superman comics. In the middle of the shelves were the stamps, mostly from faraway lands. I was most taken with the colorful triangle and circle shapes from Africa and Indonesia imprinted with elephants, giraffes, and monkeys hanging upside down from palm trees. My stamp collection was sparse, the album filled mostly with frayed and canceled stamps given to me by neighbors and my parents' friends. The brightly colored new ones were impossible to resist. Did I think that I shouldn't, that it was wrong? It's doubtful. My only concern was that I would get caught. The first time I put them in the pockets of my polka-dotted pedal pushers, I hesitated when after a few steps I heard crinkling, but by then my mother was back. I helped her unload the cart onto the cashier's counter, then walked to the door and waited, my hands deep in my pockets clutching the stamps to quiet them.

    I took more stamps each time we went shopping until the day the revolving stand was moved next to the cashier's. I didn't know why but it was clear I could no longer linger there.

    Instead, in Jumbo's toy store, close enough to ride my bike to, I moved onto Barbie and Ken doll clothes. Unlike today when many styles of the dolls were sold, in the fifties you had only one doll with multiple outfits, almost all of which I craved. The dolls did whatever I wanted and the power was heady. I'd direct them in scenarios that occupied me for hours, even strapping them onto the back of my bike to take them on a tour of my neighborhood.

The store was cluttered beyond any order, dolls jammed in among Matchbox cars, board games stacked on shelves crowded with arts and crafts. The shopkeeper resembled Santa Claus with his oversized belly and snowy hair and beard. He stayed parked on a stool behind the counter and pointed to whatever direction a toy was that his customers were seeking. My first gift to myself, for that's how I thought of it, was a sailor outfit for Ken and a swimming suit for Barbie. Over many months, my friend Lana joined me as we raided the piles for evening gowns and tuxedoes, tennis outfits with matching racquets, and a fur coat for Barbie and a trench coat for Ken. The variety expanded the possibilities of play and our imaginations ran wild as we escorted them to make-believe balls, beaches, and tennis courts.

With my mother now working full-time, I was consigned to a neighbor's home for afterschool care. Sal's wife worked as well but he was always home when my sister and I went over. I was often left alone while my sister and his daughter Babette played together in her bedroom, the door closed to me.

Sal creeped me out. Bald with thick hairy arms and a bulging belly, he was always kissing me with slobbery lips and sticking his tongue in my mouth. He did the same to my sister and we complained to my mother but nothing changed.

One day, coming from the bathroom into the hallway that led to the bedrooms, I didn't know Sal was behind me until he pushed me against the linen closet door, the bite of the doorknob bruising my spine. His pants zipper was down and he was holding something pink and squishy in his hand that he pushed into my mouth with such force that my head bounced against the wood door.

Gagging, my stomach ready to disgorge, I shoved him away to no avail. He growled like an angry dog and pinched my ears, using them to pull my head closer then back and forth until my mouth filled with hot sour liquid. What he might have said, whether or not I threw up, I don't remember.

I do remember him saying that if I told anyone what just happened, he would make sure nobody would believe me. "I'll make sure you're sent to reform school," he said, an inch away from my face.

Was it only the one time? I wasn't a secretive child; indeed, I protested loudly when I was picked on, shoved in the schoolyard, tripped when I was running, but I said nothing to my mother about this man's invasion of my mouth. Already skilled at removing myself mentally when my father's anger shook the house, I made myself forget this ever happened.

Once an adult, with children of my own, the episode resurfaced, first in my dreams, then in my conscious mind. I wasn't sure that the recollection was really true; maybe he had only put his tongue in my mouth, but the feeling of my face scraping against his hairy belly persisted until I felt compelled to take a closer look. Piecing one bit of memory with another. I knew my mouth was involved—I remembered wet—I remembered choking. One day after I dropped my older daughter off at Little League practice near my old neighborhood, on the way home, some instinct took over the steering wheel.

Four or five houses down the block, I heard screams without grasping they were mine. The car ran into the curb, jarring me back into my body, and I accelerated down that neighborhood street going close to fifty miles per hour.

It was true—I didn't make it up, it actually happened.

* * *

I was ten, in the fifth grade, when my parents betrayed me further by taking me away from the green house and my friends to live on a ridge bordering Laurel Canyon in the Hollywood Hills. My father needed to be in nature, my mother said, but also valued the proximity to downtown where most of his insurance clients worked. Carmar Drive was the only flat street surrounded by hilly avenues of fairly new homes. She pointed out that they were thinking of my sister and me, that they deliberately chose the location so we could still bicycle and skate. After spending years riding my bike to the beach and to school, I was not impressed. The street, maybe thirty houses long, didn't satisfy the adventuress I'd become. Pulled from a large elementary school with multiple classrooms for each grade, now I was in a school so tiny that only three classrooms held mixed grades and the playground was only a little larger than our backyard. Even worse, the girls who had stuck together since kindergarten didn't welcome me. This was the first time I was bullied. Mocked for my height, at least a head over most of the kids, mocked for my clumsiness, mocked for my horse-like long face, they were relentless. My mother took me into the principal's office to complain and they both came to the same conclusion.

"They wouldn't tease you if they didn't like you, Jody." I didn't believe that for a second. The girls were too vicious and the boys goaded me to crying.

"Just walk away, ignore them," the principal said. As if that would work.

I knew they were wrong, that they didn't understand how much my feelings were hurt. Not when the kids surrounded me with their taunts, putting their feet out in the aisle and on the schoolyard to trip me, not when the worst of the girls followed me into the bathroom to stand on a toilet adjacent to the stall I sat in making rude comments. Coming from a school where I was treated kindly, where my friends and I galloped around the long yard playing horses during recess, I cried every day walking up the steep street to the house, wishing I still had my underground sanctuary to hide in.

I'm sure now that the anger and sense of displacement were largely responsible for the shoplifting I returned to. My parents' treason was impossible to accept. It wasn't long after we moved that I went into a toy store near my mother's hair salon. I tried to be nonchalant as I cruised the aisles, making a mental shopping list of what I wanted. Different from Jumbo's, the shelves there were tidy, everything in its place. Finally the day came. Stashing two Barbie outfits under my jacket, I was about to walk out when I was stopped by a hand clutching my shoulder.

"What's under your jacket?" the man asked.

"Nothing," I said, believing that somehow by denying I'd taken anything, he would believe me, but no.

He unzipped my red corduroy car coat and the clothes fell to the ground. "I'm calling your parents, though I should call the police."

I thought quickly until I saw a scene from three years ago in my mind. "They're at the hospital with my grandfather who's very sick and probably going to die." I stared at my shoes.

His voice softened. "Okay, well that's too bad, but I guess I'll call after dinner. Write down your name and phone number." He thrust a pad of paper and a pencil at me.

I held onto it for a few minutes, trying to think how I could get out of it, then wrote "Joanie Foster" and changed the two sixes of my number to twos. He nodded then grabbed my shoulder again. I was afraid he'd changed his mind and was going to call the cops, but instead he said, "I know what you look like and don't ever want to see you in my store again!"

I nodded, frantic to get away, but he clutched even harder.

"You know what you've done is bad, right? That you broke the law and the police could put you in jail?" His scowl stretched from ear to ear, from nose to chin.

Shuddering, I remembered Dr. Frank, hating that she was right. As predicted, I became a criminal.

I ran down to the nail salon, wheezing breath erupting into my first full-scale asthma attack. Choked by breath I couldn't release, I slid down the tiled front of the building, my head between my knees. Black dots swarmed my vision until a lessening of pressure, like a spigot turning, slowly released the air trapped in my throat. I stayed there shaking until my mother came out. Unaware that anything unusual had happened, she scolded me for sitting on the sidewalk.

In the car next to her, I knew for sure that my luck was used up. That was it for me—no more shoplifting, never again.

4

DEFEATED

Too tall, too clumsy, too awkward. Big-boned, broad-shouldered, mouth too large. I grew so quickly that my spatial awareness couldn't keep up. I never knew where my hands were until I bumped into something or where my feet were until I tripped over somebody else's. At first glance, people defined me by my body and I hated the attention and scrutiny it brought. Being so big, there was no way to be invisible, to not be noticed. The constant comments wore on me; in an elevator, walking into a classroom on the first day of a new semester, even on the sidewalk, somebody always felt the need to comment. "My you're tall." "Hey, it's the jolly green giant." "How's the weather up there?" Worse was being called an "Amazon that belonged in a freak show," which I interpreted as having no right to breathe the same air they did. Even the teachers' aides on the playground snickered when I stumbled. A boy in the seventh grade yelled more than a few times that my large hands were perfect for hand-jobs. Not that I knew what that meant. Not then.

What I looked like bore no resemblance to the small and

timid person inside that I knew myself to be. Each time I'd catch my reflection in a store window, I was surprised anew at how large I was. By close observation of how self-confident people behaved, I worked hard at acting like I didn't care. So many adults, teachers, and others believed I was more than I was by virtue of my dissimulation, but then too often their expectations would be dashed when I couldn't maintain the performance. When they inevitably saw that I was actually an anxious, self-conscious, and insecure girl, their surprised disappointment shoved me further into self-hatred.

In 1964, the average twelve-year-old girl was 4'11". Already 5'9", I was humiliated that the world had to suffer my presence. My beautiful mother actively pursued ways to make me pretty, confirming my negative opinion about myself; otherwise, why would she try so hard to fix me? What else could I conclude, other than she didn't want to be judged a neglectful mother as she herself judged others with unattractive daughters? Each time she took me in hand, I was hopeful, although also filled with dread. From the hairdresser to the doctor to the dentist, my mother's drive to change me reinforced my certainty that I was not worth loving.

She said she wanted me to be happy, but I knew what that really meant was she wanted to be happy herself, to have a second daughter who, like my sister, would be pretty.

My mother took me to a bone doctor to see what could be done about my height and he agreed with her. I was already too tall for a girl.

"Worse, your daughter's x-rays show that she has another two or three inches to grow before reaching full height. At the very least, she'll be six feet."

"It'll be hard for her to snag a guy, being so tall. Nobody will want to dance with her," my mother said.

The doctor, more than five inches shorter than me, nodded in agreement. His face was serious, as though pondering my fate. I hated both my mother and the doctor, but hated myself more.

Neither of them looked at me or seemed to realize I was present as the doctor described a surgery that could be done to make me shorter.

"The surgery, well, it's experimental, but I just read about it in a journal. Surgeons are implanting spacers into the long bones to arrest further growth. Honestly, if she were my daughter, that's what I'd do."

When years later I told Joe about this, he was disgusted. "That's what the capitalists do, Jody. They want us to all look and act like each other, like there's some crazy standard out there for 'normal' and we must all comply. I hope you told them to fuck off."

I appreciated his defense, though I didn't dare tell him the truth—that there was nothing I wanted more than to look like a normal girl.

At dinner after the doctor's appointment, my mom told my dad about the surgery, but he shot down the idea. "It won't be covered, you can be sure, and what's the problem with being tall, anyways?" He was 6'4" and I blamed my height on him. I wished he recognized what I went through; his empathy might have lifted me from my self-loathing misery, but it wouldn't have occurred to him. Always I'd wanted somebody in my family to champion me, but that was never to be.

Then there were my teeth and lips. The dentist my mother took me to also agreed with her. My teeth were too big, my mouth too wide, my upper lip way too thin. She made me fake-laugh to show him how the lip rolled up, revealing a stripe of shiny pink gum. He shook his head as though in sorrow.

"Worse," my mother said, "her laugh is loud, too loud. I've

seen her scare people."

That was news to me, news I'd rather not have heard. Now there was something else about myself to hate.

"Nothing to do," the dentist said, "except stop laughing."

He winked at me.

Ha-ha.

The list goes on.

In the Los Angeles sixties' surf culture, straight blond hair, parted in the middle, was "the" look. My brown curly frizz bore no resemblance. In 1964, when I was twelve, Perma-Strate was advertised as the ideal hair cream especially for African-American men who wanted to "conk their kinks." My mother decided that was for me. Every few months we drove to the Crenshaw district, a predominately African-American neighborhood, to buy the hair straightener gel made from lye. It was horrid stuff, but I submitted dutifully to her combing it through my hair, never mind that I smelled like a petrochemical plant for weeks after.

My mom and I were always the only white people in the beauty supply store, which made me nervous, like we were trespassing uninvited in somebody's private home. Not my mother. She always assumed she was welcome and was well able to talk with anybody about anything.

The cream was eventually abandoned when I lost clumps of hair, but my mother had a new trick; wrapping my wet hair around two orange juice cans held with metal clips on top of my head. How I slept in those, I have no idea, but I did. In the mornings, if my hair still wasn't smooth enough, she ironed it stick-straight.

I'm making it sound like my mother was doing this to me but in truth, I cooperated fully, wanting nothing more than popular hair. And to be shorter. And to be pretty.

Then there were my feet. Nothing could fix them.

At that time the average shoe size for a girl my age was six and a half. I wore a size ten and a half. There was only one place in all of Los Angeles where a girl with a shoe size larger than nine could shop—on the third floor of Mandels in downtown Los Angeles. To reach the elevator at the back of the store, we clodhoppers were forced to walk past dozens of racks displaying hundreds of shoes, all cute and fashionable, available in every color and style. Jealousy always tightened my stomach. I wanted them all, or at the very least, to have the same choice as smaller girls.

Once, only once, when somebody she knew commented on how pretty my sister was, my mother made a point of bragging: "Jody gets all A's." The lady smiled, but even I knew that smart didn't trump pretty.

My mother made promises she shouldn't have, promises she couldn't keep. "One day you'll be beautiful." "One day you'll be happy." This was her repeated response to my chronic unhappiness and insecurity, making me believe that there would actually be a single day when I would wake up transformed into a beautiful and happy person. No gradations, no shifts, no swings. She promised, therefore it would be.

It wasn't until I was well into my twenties that I realized there would never be a "one day," that there was actually no such thing, that life didn't work that way. She lied to me, but why? Maybe she didn't know how literally I would take her. Was she trying to reassure me or comfort herself? I wish I knew.

A motley collection of journal writing from my adolescence still exists—bent and scarred spiral notebooks, wrinkled looseleaf lined papers, napkins, and recycled envelopes, all scrawled with confessions and longings. My aching need for understanding saturated the pages of my youth, yearning for social inclusion, yearning for a family whose love I could be sure of, whose protection would keep me safe. So much misery, so much hope. On one piece of paper, in tiny handwriting, I lamented my parents not caring: "When will you accept me? You never have—I'm as good now as I can be—please—what can I do?"

* * *

I was lying on the moss-green carpet in my bedroom at our new house in Laurel Canyon leafing through the latest issue of *Life* magazine. I stopped short at a photograph splashed across two pages. Smoke puffs ejected from a small airplane stretched in bubbly letters across a star and planet-filled night sky. I read the words several times trying to discern the message I knew intuitively was for me.

"*Nowhere in the universe is it written that every man, woman, and child is fated to be loved.*"

Contrary to my fantastical belief that just being alive would guaranteed love, apparently that was neither owed nor fated. Although I easily cried, that day I was dry-eyed, writing in my Barbie diary dated March 12, 1962: "Mommy hates me. Daddy does too. It's because I'm not good. I'm trying but nothing makes a difference. I'll never be good enough for her to love me like she loves my sister."

That was when I first wrote about the two me's—the one watching and judging myself, the other the person I projected hoping people would only see how together I was and not the messy me inside. I wrote: "People see me, they think they know me, but they only see what I choose to reveal. I mirror them in response to their confidences. They think me so special, when in truth, I'm hollow, filled only with who's in front of me at the moment."

5
AWAKENED

I can say that my interest in politics was my own, but being a liberal Democrat was as much a part of my family DNA as being Jewish. Politics were often the main discussion at our dinner table, my parents sharing with each other the news of the day gleaned from the *Los Angeles Times* and radio talk shows. My impression was that the main attraction of the Democratic Party was their stance on social services and objection to state rule over federal. I don't recall them ever discussing the larger agenda of racism or poverty, which later made me think these were issues they didn't care about, but I really don't know. Their relationship was one of mutual respect and appreciation, and more than a few times I listened to them debating about a measure on the ballot until they found common ground.

They were especially excited about John Kennedy. His charismatic youth and liberal agenda, as well as his beautiful wife and children, appealed to them, and my parents' enthusiasm was infectious. My father predicted Kennedy would lead us forward, that he could unstick the country from the political morass of the Cold War and stagnant economy.

On a school day, I was home sick with a stomach virus and snuggled in a blanket on my mother's bed, watching the sitcom *Pete and Gladys*, when a newsman interrupted the programming:

PRESIDENT KENNEDY HAS BEEN ASSASSINATED

I shouted for my mother, my voice already cracking in a rush of sobs. She ran in wearing the gingham yellow apron with blue rickrack that she had sewed herself, still holding the dishtowel and soup ladle she was drying. I pointed at the television and knew the instant she comprehended what had just happened. The blood literally drained from her face. Scooting to the edge of the bed to get closer to the set, she sat down next to me. I wrapped my arms around her so tightly that her heart beating hard against mine could have been my own.

In the Cold War fifties and sixties, on the last Friday of each month, a citywide air raid siren sounded at ten a.m., the signal to duck under our school desks and cover our heads against nuclear bombs. We didn't take it too seriously. The practice gave us an opportunity to be silly, to poke the person next to us, to write stupid things on the linoleum floor. I was too young to understand the threat but was still subliminally aware of the pervasive fear, much talked about between my mother and her friends. Black and white pictures of mushroom clouds haunted my dreams. I'd wake screaming, twisted and sweating in my sheets, much like I would for years following that night we armed ourselves in my living room.

I was again watching television in my parents' room when

the news came that three voter registrars, two Jews and an African-American, were found murdered in Philadelphia, Mississippi, presumably by members of the KKK and the city police department. They were working in an especially impoverished area where many citizens had never voted. Overwhelmed by the sudden realization that there truly were hate-mongers that could kill with impunity, I especially mourned the death of Andrew Goodman, his last name the same as my maternal grandfather.

How could this be? Why were so many people so poor and disenfranchised? Why was it so hard for people of color to have the same opportunities as white? Who was in charge? Why were wealthy people so reluctant to share? I asked my mother to explain, I demanded she tell me why, but she could only shrug and say, "That's just the way things are."

Not good enough, I remember thinking, it's just not right. I would think that again and again, not knowing then that I was already on the path toward the politics I would eventually embrace in the Revolutionary Union.

I was eleven in 1963. A little while after President Kennedy was assassinated my mother took my sister and me to the Hollywood Bowl to see Bob Dylan. Thinking he was just another peace folksinger like Joan Baez or Maryanne Faithful, she was not at all prepared for his snarly voice that spoke to me in a way I'd never experienced before. He knew my hurting heart; he knew my sad soul.

My mom and sister complained about his grating tone, my mother unhappy that his songs were more rebellious than sweet. I wanted them to shut up. Didn't they realize they were in the presence of greatness? They wanted to leave at intermission. I refused.

Then toward the end he sang "Ballad of a Thin Man," about

the pressure on one person to be like another and to be a more worthy person, which in reality translated as more wealthy and conforming. To those in my generation, the mainstream was synonymous with the "establishment," another disparaging word for both those in authority and those who adhered to what was considered an antiquated morality.

Bob Dylan pulled me over the fence I'd chafed against for years, forever separating me from my unsympathetic parents and the world they inhabited. When the song ended, I looked around and saw others similarly dazed. Where within my family I was always so alone, there at the Hollywood Bowl I saw others ready to abandon phoniness, greed, and moralizing, people who believed more in love than materialism. I found my people, all of us a generation of alienated hearts.

After the concert I walked to the car ten feet behind my mother and sister, cherishing the newfound realization that my mother's constant admonitions to be more like my sister were meaningless, that it wasn't me who was wrong. It was them.

That night changed my world from the lonely angst of pre-Dylan to the excitement and inclusivity of post-Dylan, from a world of self-loathing solitude to a world of infinite possibility. To the future I had within me to define myself as separate from my parents, to my perennial search for a new family of people I could feel a part of. Indeed, a tribe was what I craved, and what I would find in the Revolutionary Union with Joe as my partner.

I was in the eighth grade when Watts, an impoverished African-American community east of downtown Los Angeles, erupted into a riot when a cop tried to arrest a Black man for drunk driving.

Charges of police brutality were shouted, storefronts shattered, goods looted, the municipality illuminated by blazing fires. On the television I saw a too-skinny Black woman leaving a market struggling to maneuver two carts stacked high with packages of Pampers. The mainstream press roundly condemned the looters, especially those filmed loading up television sets and record players in the backs of vans. Still, that woman with her baby's diapers was the only person I saw. She grabbed my heart and I hoped she was okay.

On the third and last day of the riots, I cut class and hitchhiked to Watts with an African-American girlfriend who, like me, was middle-class. Cindy sat behind me in our eighth grade algebra class and we helped each other the best we could through the mysteries of solving x and y. Did she initiate our quest or did I? I only remember that we were curious. Three rides later, we were east of downtown when an elderly Black man pulled over. It was a hot scorching Monday.

"Where you chicks going?" he asked. I liked the way he said "chicks"—it made me feel cool.

"Watts," Cindy said as we got into his car.

"No way, are you crazy? Does your mama know where you at?" He turned the car around to get on the Santa Monica freeway going west, insisting he take us home, all the way scolding us for our stupidity and ignorance.

"Did you think you were going to a party?" he asked.

No, not a party, but a place that felt important for us to witness. I couldn't explain it beyond that.

6
LOVING

In the early years of my adolescence, I didn't yet know that I was a minuscule drop in a groundswell of the sixties' rebellion, one part in millions of a generation disgusted by the materialism of our parents and societal rules that valued conformity and wealth over humanity and love.

"Love is all you need," sang the Beatles. A cliché now, but my reality in the mid to late 1960s when the Sunset Strip in West Hollywood became the epicenter of new happenings, drugs, and the sexual revolution, where young people were breaking previously enshrined cultural norms and mores. Boys with long hair and girls with flowers painted on their cheeks flashed peace signs on the sidewalks and from their cars. They leaned out the windows of their beat-up vehicles with plates from Idaho, Ohio, or Kansas to ask, "Where's it at?" That was the question of our times, all of us seekers for a life where love was the valued currency. We wanted the world to be different, to treat us differently, and we were young and idealistic enough to believe that we could make it happen.

Annoyed with the nightly auto and pedestrian traffic congestion caused by the curious, local residents and businesses along the Strip protested to the city, prompting them to impose a ten p.m. curfew for those under eighteen. A Public Service Announcement was broadcast on every television and radio channel, usually with an emergency signal preceding.

"It's ten p.m. Do you know where your children are?"

I was fourteen in 1966 when I ventured to the Strip for the first time. Underage, I couldn't go to the clubs, but hung out with friends to check out the scene. That night, at fifteen minutes past ten, the West Hollywood police swept up anyone who looked younger than eighteen into police transport buses. Excited to be part of the unruly crowd, I was also anxious about my parents. They thought I was attending a Jewish study group for teens that a friend of mine belonged to.

Once the bus got to the station, the boys with long hair were pulled aside and given buzz cuts by the police. Their pale necks and cheeks was a sad thing to see.

I had no choice but to give my phone number to a cop who told me he would call my parents to pick me up. It was a zoo in the front room, kids and parents all trying to find each other, some of the kids crying, others yelling in anger. It took about thirty minutes for my father to come. I saw him first, his eyes scanning the room, his mouth a grimace of disdain I knew well.

As I made my way toward him, my father gestured to one of the officers.

"I'm looking for my daughter," I heard him say.

"Dad, I'm here." I tapped him on the shoulder.

He turned quickly, his hand fisted, poised to strike. The policeman grabbed it and said something too quietly for me to hear. Whatever it was, my dad dropped his arm and I let go of the breath I didn't know I was holding.

"Let's go. Your mother is waiting in the car." He spat the words and I felt them land in my chest as harshly as he intended.

"It isn't fair, Dad, I wasn't doing anything wrong!" I hated how like a child I sounded.

"Life isn't fair, Jody. I thought you'd know that by now." Or that's what I wished he'd said—it might have tempered my expectations. As it was, fighting for fairness would define me for years to come.

The Strip exploded in riots protesting the police round-ups. Thousands were busted. A manager of many popular L.A. bands was noted as saying: "If you had to put your finger on an event that was a barometer of the tide turning, it would probably be the Sunset Strip riots."

By the end of the ninth grade, I was smoking a joint most mornings before class. Formerly a straight A student, my highest grade that year was a C. The many unsatisfactories in work habits and cooperation on my semester-end report card gave credence to my distraction and rebellion.

In the tenth grade, I met with my counselor. In her cubicle, Mrs. Uribe asked, "Where do you see yourself once you graduate?"

"College," I said, without hesitation. UC Berkeley was my intended destination, the university where my greatly admired older cousin attended.

She shook her head. Was that a look of pity she gave me? "I don't think so. We have you on the trade track, not the college track. The only way you'll get to college is to completely change your behavior and, frankly, Jody, I don't think you have the intelligence it would take."

How dare she tell me what I could or could not do? Still, I heeded her advice and became much better at controlling my behavior in class once I stopped smoking pot before school.

* * *

January 28, 1967: Happy fifteenth birthday to me! My good friend Linda stuck fifteen candles into a cheeseburger purchased at Handy's, a corner hamburger stand in West Hollywood. It was where the kids from the local Catholic school who transferred into my junior high school in the ninth grade hung out. Already having sex and smoking pot, going to school when they wanted, cutting when they didn't, it was these boys and girls to whom I was drawn, by whom I wanted to be accepted. The boys were so very cool, mostly Italian-American—their hair just a bit longer than the dress code allowed, leather jackets, tight T-shirts. The girls wore short skirts and tight tops, lipstick and purple or blue eye shadow. So hip, so groovy, I thought.

Linda's gift was a sugar cube of the Owsley LSD prevalent at the time. I let it dissolve on my tongue, feeling ice and then heat pour through my veins. Shivering and sweating at the same time, hyperconscious of my breathing, for a moment panicking that I'd forgotten how. I concentrated: inhale, exhale, inhale, exhale. Colors highlighted the words my fingers traced on the scarred top of the metal café table where I sat.

"Love," I wrote, 'love, love, we all need love.' Scratches on the white painted surface wiggled, looking like ripples of water in a frenetic wind.

The kaleidoscopic world around me sparkled fresh and new. I stood up only to put another dime in the jukebox, playing the same song, over and over: Simon and Garfunkel's "For Emily, Wherever I May Find Her." The melody carried me higher yet, and I knew the ballad would mean something more in my life. More than seventeen years later, I named my first daughter Emily to honor its profound beauty.

I was happy, so happy, so in love with love. Linda and I visited one friend, stayed there awhile, then visited another. I flopped onto front lawns, tripping on the colors and pulsating hallucinations. What a relief to be out of my body. As the day waned, so did the high, and I couldn't wait to trip again.

My fifteenth year was even more significant in my expanding political consciousness as well as my growing activism. On June 23, 1967, President Lyndon Johnson came to Los Angeles for a $1,000/plate—equivalent to $7,500 in 2017—fundraiser for the Democratic Party, staged at the Century City Hotel in midtown Los Angeles. It was the last day of the tenth grade, but two friends and I ditched to join more than eleven thousand marching from the Federal building in Westwood to the hotel chanting: *Hey, hey, LBJ, how many kids did you kill today?*

Being one of so many people made me feel vital to the larger cause that tied us all together and there was nowhere else I'd rather be. The three of us were walking somewhere in the middle of the crowd when the march abruptly stopped. We didn't know yet that a cordon of policemen wielding nightsticks was pushing back the people in front. We, and those behind us, were soon jammed in so tightly that we could neither move sideways or backward. Teargas cylinders were pitched into the crowd, exploding smoke when they hit the ground. People panicked, climbing over each other to escape the fumes and the cops working their way through the throng flailing batons. My chest tightened, my eyes watered and burned, as my second asthma attack crested, dropping me to my knees. Marchers surged around me, their legs making a cage I couldn't escape from until a woman's strong arm pulled me up and half dragged, half walked me to the grassy median on the periphery of the chaotic crowd. My savior alerted a young man with a Red Cross armband who slapped an oxygen mask on my face until my breathing finally normalized.

Most of those marching that day were white liberals intent on raising political consciousness across Los Angeles. The prime-time networks were there when two policemen beat up a white woman. It was a breaking story supplanting all other programming. I couldn't help but wonder if it would have been such urgent news if she were Black.

My mother and her friends finally woke up and joined an organization called "Another Mother For Peace." She wore a pendant engraved with these words: *"War is not healthy for children and other living things,"* and brought home a leather peace sign for my father to wear. He didn't, but after he died I was surprised and pleased to find he'd kept it in the top drawer of his dresser next to his cufflinks, tiepins, and underwear.

That was the year I joined thousands at the Los Angeles Forum for a Joan Baez concert. Toward the end, a trashcan on stage was lit on fire while Ms. Baez called for boys to bring up their draft cards. As they walked, one by one, down the aisles toward her, I was crying, everybody was, while we swayed with linked arms and sang "We Shall Overcome."

Polarizing me further was the news in April broadcasting from Columbia University in New York City. Students were occupying the administration buildings in protest of the university plan to expand into Black-owned Harlem. The cameras were in the middle of it, and so was the television audience, as the NYPD rousted the strikers with tear gas and clubs. But this wasn't Watts where impoverished people of color were regularly targets of police brutality but an Ivy League university where white privileged students were getting beaten and jailed. An internal civil war was brewing in the country, not just between Black and White, or rich and poor, but those for and against peace, those for and against institutional racism and economic disparity.

In January 1968, the North Vietnamese communist troops launched the Tet Offensive against U.S. and South Vietnamese troops. Its success sent waves of shock and discontent across the home front, sparking the most intense period of anti-war protests to date. By early February, a Gallup poll showed only 35 percent of the population approved of Johnson's handling of the war and a full 50 percent disapproved (the rest had no opinion). Joining the anti-war demonstrations were members of the organization Vietnam Veterans Against the War, founded by a former Marine, Ron Kovic, who was wounded and paralyzed in the war.

Many, including him, were in wheelchairs and on crutches. The sight of these men on television throwing away the medals they had won did much to win the population over to the anti-war cause.

Now, three years after the United States entered the Vietnam War, Walter Cronkite, America's beloved and respected anchorman and an early advocate of the war, visited Indochina and was forever changed by what he observed. Stunned by the damage his country perpetuated in their civil war, he urged immediate negotiation between the United States and North Vietnamese armies.

Watching him on CBS with my parents, I could see they were flustered. Both moved from their comfortable seats against the pillows at the head of the bed to sit on the edge next to me. My father nodded as though he knew all along the inevitable failure in the Vietnam War. This statement from the journalist they tuned to nightly for trusted information shook their world. Suddenly it was acceptable, even respectable, for Americans of all classes and color to protest the war.

As the movement grew, it came to include support for civil rights and the ripening women's liberation movement, along with opposition to racism and nuclear weaponry. The protest movement in the United States joined international opposition against the war, especially in London, Paris, Berlin, and Rome. Hundreds of thousands demonstrating in Europe marched not only to object to the Vietnam War, but also against state repression in their own countries. Ten thousand students in Berlin held a sit-in; London police injured more than eighty protesters and arrested close to two hundred of its citizens; Japanese students fought against the presence of U.S. soldiers stationed there on American bases. American conscientious objectors crossed the border into Canada. The international support did much to lift the spirits of the millions of Americans already marching against the war.

By then I was on the streets, an avid war protester. The civil rights movement and Martin Luther King Jr.'s message of nonviolence particularly resonated with me—I put up a poster of him on my blue bedroom wall.

He ignited the spark for future activism. I loved the inclusiveness of being one of so many, all of us together for the singular purpose of ending the despised and despicable war in Vietnam. It became common knowledge that the war was not, as the government claimed, fought to defeat the domino communist effect in Indochina, but for the oil reserves that the land was rich in. On the streets, marching, chanting, and waving homemade signs gave me a high that I would feel many more times during my time in San Jose and again, not so long ago, at the Women's

March in Los Angeles after Donald Trump, whose policies parallel many of the Vietnam era, was elected president.

Both Dr. King and presidential candidate Robert F. Kennedy were assassinated that year as the horrors of the undeclared Vietnam War continued to be broadcast daily on televisions across the nation. Journalists also gave witness to race riots in Newark and Detroit. Every night before bed, I sat on the floor in my parents' room, squeezed into the narrow space between their king-sized bed and the bureau in the open closet where our only television sat. I watched the daily skirmishes in faraway jungles and on our city streets. The images assaulted me, and I sat there blown away by the brutal treatment done to the Vietnamese civilians by American soldiers, and to Black people on the streets by the police and National Guard.

How could I not be radicalized?

7
CONFLICTED

The summer of 1968 had been deemed the "Summer of Love." I was one in the crowds surging into Griffith Park for the weekly love-ins where local bands like the Byrds, Mamas and Papas, Love, and the Doors played for free. Joints passed from one to another, most of us wearing multi-colored beaded necklaces and bracelets. I'd never felt better as I twirled and leapt in improvised dance moves alongside hundreds of partners. Timothy Leary, an early proponent of psychedelics, invited us to get high and unite against the establishment. The concept of free love gave definition to the counterculture movement as young people celebrated their rejection of acquiescence and the outmoded morality of the fifties.

At my third or fourth love-in, I met a man somewhere in his twenties named Spoon. I went with him to his apartment where he took my virginity on a stained mattress in a Hollywood squat. Most of the kids I hung out with were already having sex and I didn't like being the only virgin in the crowd. I'd fantasized about sex for years, and my inexperience had come to feel like a burden, like something I was missing out on and had to get behind me.

Spoon reassured me that he'd done this before, claiming that relieving virgins of their hymens was something he was good at. He placed books under the back legs of his bed, tilting us into what he called an advantageous position for deflowering. I lay underneath him, arms and legs splayed, staring at the Playboy centerfold on the ceiling of a buxom redhead with red pubic hair. Minutely aware of each move he made, I only wanted it to be over. Spoon made no effort to arouse me or even wet his way in. The pain was a shock. I didn't know it would hurt. I cried out, exciting him to buck harder until finally he finished with heavy sighs and groans.

I hated it but was also relieved. Mission accomplished. That night I looked in the mirror, marveling that I looked no different than the day before. A line had been crossed, a milestone achieved. There would no longer be a reason to say no to the boys who claimed to want me. I marked the day in my diary with the words "all no's will be yeses from this day on."

It would turn out that the next few times I had sex while still in high school were also alienating experiences, and whether that was because I went to bed with boys in absence of a relationship or because I wasn't yet physically mature, I'm not sure. Probably both were true. Indeed, it wouldn't be until I met Joe when I was seventeen that I first felt lust, that my body craved entry.

As graduation from high school neared, my reckless behavior began to scare me—sleeping with men I'd known for an hour, hitchhiking alone, dipping regularly into a friend's stash of speed, recovering from a day taking uppers with downers to sleep at night.

Caught in the crosshairs of my mother's expectations and

her chronic disappointment, I came to believe that if I didn't get away from her, I might self-destruct. Trying and failing to please her cemented me to the dregs of Hollywood rather than en route to college. Still, my careless actions challenged my sense of self-preservation. I was making impulsive decisions from a place of rage, consciously defying fear by telling myself that being scared was not a good enough reason to hold back. It didn't occur to me, not then, that fear could be a positive warning not to be ignored.

I made a plan with a friend who found an apartment in Hollywood for us but I was afraid to tell my parents, afraid they wouldn't allow me to move out—at seventeen I was still legally underage. I thought our talking together with Dr. Anderson, the psychologist my mother had me seeing, might be the best option. It was a tense session, me trying to say what I needed to say, but hyperaware of my father's narrowed eyes, his mouth rimmed white with tension.

"How will you support yourself?" he asked. "We sure as hell aren't going to give you any money. Are you still going to college?"

Only that morning I had received acceptances to several state colleges. It turned out my counselor was right—I didn't have the grades for Berkeley. San Jose State, close to San Francisco, appealed to me for no other reason than it was furthest from Los Angeles.

I took a big breath. My voice shook. "Of course I'm going to college and I'm already registered with a temporary agency for the summer. They've already got several clerical jobs lined up for me."

I stood up, hoping to be bigger than I felt.

"This is bullshit," my father said. His words charged my adrenaline, the extra heat made my temper boil over.

"You should know. You're full of it!"

I can still see him lifting from his chair, his fist balled. He struck fast, the blow glancing off my shoulder since I was also in motion, running for the door, then down the stairs from the third to the second to the first floor. It was dusk outside, the street lights just coming on. I started walking, not sure what to do or where to go. I'd left my jacket and purse behind, not even a dime to call a friend, let alone a quarter for the bus. Santa Monica Blvd, in West Hollywood, was a busy thoroughfare during the day, but few cars were out at night. I stuck out my thumb, but then pulled it back when the first passing car slowed—I felt too vulnerable, too close to tears. Instead, I kept walking northeast toward the house in Laurel Canyon more than eight miles away, keeping to the shadows, stopping occasionally to rest on bus benches. Anger first steered me, but I was afraid and alone and so cold. It took more than two hours to reach the corner bus stop where my mother usually picked me up. Living in the mountains was horrible for a teenager. It wasn't on a bus route, and I had to depend on my parents to drive me up and down the hill.

I checked the coin return slot of the phone booth outside the corner pharmacy and lucked out—two dimes. My father answered before the first ring finished.

"Where are you?" I hated that I needed him to rescue me, but I was too exhausted by then to walk up the steep and winding hills to our house.

"Sunset and Fairfax."

He hung up and I didn't know if that meant he was coming to get me or not. Twenty minutes later he drove up, reached across to open the passenger door, and I got in.

I said nothing, neither did he. In front of the house that I'd long despised, he let me out before pulling into the garage. I went directly to the bathroom, then to my room to crawl into bed fully clothed. No recriminations, no attempts at reconciliation. Nothing more was said about my moving out.

High school graduation was three days later. The next morning, I packed a suitcase, grabbed my pillow and my toothbrush, and left the house without a word to anyone. My friend Denise, who would be my roommate, was already waiting in her station wagon to pick me up.

She had found a studio apartment in a Spanish colonial courtyard. It was in the heart of Hollywood on Fountain Ave., a busy cross street of similar apartments and duplexes. The managers, Ranger and Kitten, were straight out of central casting: biker and biker chick. Both obese with long snarled blond hair, their arms heavily tattooed. They wore jean jackets, the sleeves ripped off, Diablo Devils embroidered on the front and back.

We discovered our apartment crawling with hundreds of humongous cockroaches. That first night we slept on Ranger and Kitten's living room floor. When my mother came to visit the next day, bringing us towels and egg salad sandwiches, she took one horrified look at the place and rushed out to purchase a newspaper. Within hours she helped us move into a one-bedroom furnished apartment just a few miles further into Hollywood. Once again, my mother rescued me. I was embarrassed but also relieved.

Nail heads popped through scuffed wood floors. Faded gold brocade hung loosely over the windows. Painted white with grease stains over the stove, the kitchen had few utensils—two plates, two bowls, two spoons, two knives, two forks, and one pot, one pan. The building, likely built in the 1920s, was old Hollywood—beige stucco with a double-wide gated entry capped with cast-iron letters: *Waring Manor*.

Through the temp agency, I found work as a typist in downtown Los Angeles. Since I could work as much or little as I pleased, I barely made it in more than three days a week, too busy getting high with the many friends who still lived with their parents and saw my place as their personal get-away. Not that I minded—I was the popular one now, a flip to the script. Even the boy who teased me so mercilessly in junior high about my big hands apologized one night, saying he had no idea how cool I was.

Yeah, I was cool. So cool that I had no idea how to take care of myself, no skills to self-regulate. At home my mother still cleaned up after me, still did my laundry, still made my bed. I knew how to vacuum, iron, and wash and dry dishes, but had no idea how to cook an egg, grocery shop, or wash my clothes. I didn't think to wear a coat when it was cold outside—my mother always stood at the door holding one out for me. Expecting myself to be self-reliant, it was a harsh lesson to realize how much of my thinking my mother had done for me.

That was another summer of drugs. Acid dropped at least twice a week, bong hits daily. I shot up heroin twice. Nothing had ever felt so good. Too good. After the second time, fear clenched my stomach when I came down. I liked it too much and knew that if I shot up just one more time, I'd never want to stop.

Again, I saw two possibilities in my future—one to end up a junkie dead in an alley, or two, never use a needle again. To this day, more than forty-five years later, the lift-off and high remain a visceral memory, the swell of joy pulsing through my veins, all hurt tenderized by the opiate.

* * *

The summer ended. My roommate's sister moved in while I packed my father's car with my blue bike and boxes of clothes and books for the drive to San Jose. Finally I was going to college. The day marked the beginning of something I never could have anticipated—my transition from sixties love child to a communist who slept with guns under my bed and a poster of Joseph Stalin taped on the wall above my pillow.

8

ROUSED

I'd always seen college as a get-out-of-childhood card. Even when I was getting high and skipping classes in high school, I pictured my future self sitting in a circle of intelligent boys and girls generating heat in our discussion of literature and politics in a world far away from the drugs and random sex of my Hollywood adolescence.

But in the fall of 1969, the fantasy of being part of a collegial and erudite world was dashed within a week of my first semester at San Jose State University. Ready to be serious, to use my mind that already felt like a flaccid muscle wasted away from the pot, speed, and quantities of LSD I'd consumed, most of the girls I met were only excited to be away from home, eager to drink and get high for the first time, and the boys no different from the druggy unmotivated guys in Hollywood that I'd been happy to leave behind. Too many of them were enrolled on the student draft-deferment track, giving them license to prolong their adolescent partying while their parents supported them for as long as the war in Vietnam continued.

In those early days as a freshman, I was lonely, disappointed, and disoriented, seeing no place for me to fit. I had smoked a few cigarettes in Los Angeles, but in those early days in San Jose I began buying packs of Marlboros just for an excuse to sit on various benches on campus for the purpose of lighting up, hoping somebody would come along and recognize me as a kindred spirit. That didn't happen, but I did get to know the sprawling campus that was the founding college of the California State University system. The prettiest buildings were overlaid with ivy, the lawns immaculate, the trees luxurious in their foliage.

Alerted by a leaflet handed out in the student quad four weeks into the semester, I attended an anti-war rally on campus. Interest propelled me, but even more, I hoped to meet people like me—sensitive to injustice, angry about the war in Vietnam and with the ruling establishment—people who wanted to use their thinking minds to effect change.

Only the day before the rally, disturbing news made the headlines. William Calley, the U.S. Army lieutenant originally sentenced to life in prison after the soldiers under his command decimated My Lai, a village in South Vietnam, would only serve two years under house arrest. More than six hundred unarmed civilians—mostly women, children, and old men—were massacred. While fires ravaged the small village, women were gang-raped and children mutilated. Enraged, my feelings of helpless impotency made me even more determined to find radical solutions. There must be something I could do.

That afternoon about a dozen of us crowded close to the makeshift stage in the center of the campus on a large concrete slab edged by yellowed grass. The October sun was sweltering, overheating me in my white cotton blouse and cut-off blue jeans. One boy in particular stood out from the other speakers with his short hair, sweat-stained white V-neck T-shirt, faded Levis, and leather oxfords. Introducing himself as Joe, he bore no resemblance to the previous overwrought longhaired and bearded speechmakers who ranted against the war but offered no solutions. I craved calm intelligence, coherent strategies, and intentional ambition, all that Joe seemed to embody.

With great eloquence, he spun a cohesive argument holding the American capitalist corporations responsible for the Vietnam War—indeed, for all of the world's evil.

"It's their relentless drive for profit, using imperialism as their vehicle, that are bombing the innocent and sending our soldiers off to die in a country whose business we have no right to interfere with!"

His words struck a chord deep within me. I was already alerted to the scourge of imperialism, although I didn't yet know the word, during a trip to Disneyland when I was fifteen. On the ride "It's A Small World," international village people sang to us merrily along our way. Our car reached the exit to be greeted by a slowly spinning oversized globe with American flags stuck in every nation. A banner sign proclaimed, "The Bank of America is Everywhere!" How dare they, I thought, how fucking dare they. I was a one-woman boycott against the park and the Bank of America from that day on. Several years later, when students at the University of California at Santa Barbara burned down a branch of the bank in protest, my friends and I cheered.

Listening to Joe, I comprehended that rather than amorphous and multiple enemies too many to take on, there were only the twinned swords of capitalism and imperialism. I was inspired, confident that the devil that could be named could be defeated. If Joe was right, if those swords were crushed, then one day we would live in peace, one day nobody would be hungry, wealth would be shared, and all would live a better life. Fueled by his enthusiasm, his words gave me hope when I truly needed it.

Always attracted to articulate speakers and good-looking men, I approached Joe after his speech, having no idea that that would be the first step of what became more than three years of my life committed to the Communist ideology of Karl Marx, Vladimir Lenin, and Mao Tse-Tung. Jittery with excitement and anticipation, I introduced myself to him by the side of the stage. I don't remember whose suggestion it was, but we walked together to the student union and sat with coffee at a dark wood table scratched with innocuous graffiti—hearts surrounding a boy and girl's name, *forever* written just below, a few peace signs, and rows of numbers from someone likely using the table as a calculator. Mid-afternoon, it was sparsely filled with students, most with creased brows gazing down at open books, pen or pencil in hand.

Joe told me right away that he was a member of the Revolutionary Union, a regional Communist organization. "Our purpose is to educate and mobilize the working class to revolt against capitalism." He sounded like a commercial, but when he went on to explain the history of the group, he had my rapt attention.

"It's only a year old and came out of the student anti-war movement. In 1968, veterans of the Communist Party, Students for a Democratic Society, and Bay Area radicals formed the RU, our intention to model Maoism in China."

"Why China?" I asked. I knew next to nothing about the country, so far away.

"We see the rule of China as a militant revolutionary force considerably to the left of the revisionist Russian bureaucracy, and anticipate that capitalism will be replaced by socialism in ten, fifteen years tops. All before we're thirty."

He smiled; I shook my head in wonder. Revisionism? Russia? Communist Party? I didn't understand any of it, but I didn't ask for explanations, at least not that afternoon. Instead, I wanted to listen, to let his words flow uninterrupted.

He explained that in the South and East Bay, including Palo Alto, Richmond, and San Jose, there were student, community, and worker collectives within the Revolutionary Union, and that most of the members operated within organizations like anti-war coalitions and unions.

"Our ideology has tactics and strategies toward the day when all that is wrong will be set right." If not said exactly, that's what I heard. Wrongs will be set right. He pretty much had me there. Me seventeen, him eighteen, both so very serious, our intentions for a just world heartfelt.

Joe sucked down unfiltered cigarettes, not noticing when they burned his yellowed fingers. I drew deeply on one, then another Marlboro. My face felt elastic, responding more to Joe's presence than just to what he was saying. Forehead wrinkled, empathetic frowns, eyebrows drawn up, nodding at just the right times while I tried to make sense of the volume of words he threw out. I was interested in the ideology he described, but I was also a girl struck by a boy.

We left behind a Styrofoam cup close to full with the dregs of our cigarettes. Joe walked me to my dorm and gave my hand a brief squeeze before taking off.

Still buzzing, I went upstairs to my room in Hoover Hall. The dormitory was a same-sex, squat two-story brick building. Residents signed in and out at the front desk and shared one bathroom and a single payphone per wing. Boys were allowed only in the common space downstairs; they had to be gone by ten p.m. on weeknights, midnight on weekends. The outside doors locked at eleven during the week and if we didn't make it back by then it was noted with a red demerit on our record. I thought all this laughable. My mother, however, was thrilled. Although she should have known better, she assumed that all these rules would keep me under control.

I shared a room on the second floor with a girl named Mary, a devout Christian from Sacramento. I found her sitting on her bed scribbling math equations into a red wire-bound notebook. We were still shy with each other, careful not to get in each other's way. She glanced up when I came in and waved her pencil at me, her face pinched and weary. I thought her comical in her pink baby-doll pajamas, similar to ones I wore when I was eight.

When I saw the posters she had put up over her bed while I was out, I nearly gagged. Donny Osmond, Paul McCartney, and the Monkees in positions mirroring mine of Bob Dylan, Joan Baez, and Janis Joplin. AM vs. FM, pop vs. folk and rock. We couldn't have been more different.

"I got the top grade in calculus but this makes no sense!" Mary's wire-rimmed glasses sat crooked on her nose.

"Wish I could help but I barely passed geometry the second time around. Have you left the room at all today? Have you eaten?" The cafeteria was a few buildings away and not a place either of us would go in pajamas.

She shook her head, her normally squeaky clean brown hair falling uncombed over her eyes.

"Come on." I grabbed our towels. "We both need showers, then we'll eat."

Mary and I shared her shampoo and conditioner and went for dinner together. With too many choices, I piled food on my plate enough for two people. My stomach always flat, I would soon gain the proverbial freshman fifteen pounds but I wasn't thinking of that then. Instead, memories of what Joe had said scurried through my mind. I was excited by what might lie ahead: Joe, yes, but also the Revolutionary Union's prescription for peace. Justice was what I truly cared about and it felt personal to me that so many were under the thumb of an avaricious government owned by corporate wealth.

The next day, already late for class, I found Joe lingering outside my dorm, the remnants of several cigarettes on the brick walkway at his feet. I ran my fingers through my hair, ran my tongue over dry lips, and covered my wide-open smile with the palm of my hand as my mother often admonished me to do.

"Hi," he said.

"What are you doing here?"

"Just hanging around." He looked everywhere but at me while I kept my eyes fixed on a point just past his shoulder. "Where's your first class?"

I was enrolled in an honors seminar-based Humanities program, a new experiment by higher educational institutes meant to facilitate greater class participation. The class sat in a circle rather than in rows of desks, now not so unusual, but in 1969 still a novel concept. What might have been riveting was made impossibly boring by the professor, a Brylcreemed older man who always wore the same ill-fitting three-piece pinstriped suit. He preferred telling us about his European travels instead of following the more interesting syllabus.

Joe and I walked across the street toward the classroom when he took my hand. "Never mind going to class. My car's not too far. Let's go." His touch was sweet—I didn't think twice.

Mid-autumn, the campus was still summer-parched, the morning sun beaming hot from the east. Our reflection in a window showed an odd couple, at least to me—he in an un-buttoned un-ironed denim shirt over a white t-shirt, hardy work boots worn down on the outer heels, and short trimmed brown hair; me in my usual bell-bottoms and beaded moccasins, topped by a head of Jewish curly frizz. He was my height, maybe an inch taller, hard to tell since we both slouched.

Little was said, even while he led me several blocks from campus to his 1950's Chevrolet Cavalier. Driving down San Carlos Blvd., Joe stretched his right arm along the edge of the blue plastic bench seat, tempting me to move closer, to press my hips against his. We might have gone to a Fosters Freeze, or maybe that was another time. I no longer recall the specifics, though I can still summon up my excitement. His attention was unexpected and I thrilled to it. He could have taken me anywhere.

We talked about the latest action of the Weather Underground, a far more radical group than the RU. They had just bombed a statue of a policeman in Chicago, erected in 1886, in honor of officers slain during a workers' strike for an eight-hour workday. The event eventually led to the naming of May 1 as International Workers' Day.

"What do you think?" he asked, about the Weathermen's action.

"I don't know much about them. But what's the point of destroying a statue from more than eighty years ago?"

"It's symbolic, a way to remind people of the early labor movement. The strikers back then were only fighting for decent work conditions but the system plowed them down. It all comes down to the scourge of capitalism that exploits workers."

"So you support them then, the Weathermen?"

"Yes and no. Ultimately they're anarchists with no theory or clear agenda. Their actions certainly won't mobilize the working class which is most critical to a successful revolution." Then he added, "Still, I'm pretty impressed by their convictions."

Lying in my narrow dorm bed that night, I was tired but too

wound-up to sleep. Instead, I sat up against my pillow and wrote in my journal. Many years later, when I again read that page, I was surprised to see that I'd only written about Joe and not at all about the political ideology that we spent most of the day talking about.

The next Saturday, Joe picked me up to drive south on the 101 to the Santa Cruz boardwalk. I'd brought mescaline. Even though I wanted nothing more to do with the drug scene in LA, I still liked how good being high made me feel.

He was both surprised and intrigued. "Really? Where'd you get it?"

"A girl in my Spanish class. You in?"

"Sure, should be fun." He took my hand, pulling me closer.

Once at the boardwalk, we chased down the mescaline with fresh-squeezed orange juice bought from a fruit stand. Giggling as the drug worked its way through our bloodstream, we went from game to game in the arcade—ball in the basket, bottle stand, the water gun. Joe won a purple rabbit at the skeet table and gave it to a little girl watching from nearby. We rode on the merry-go-round, him on an appaloosa, me on a pinto, holding hands while the horses slid up and down the rails.

The main attraction was the Big Dipper, a rickety wooden roller coaster built in 1924. The line was long and while we waited, I watched it closely, anticipating the stomach drops as the cars slowly, slowly, chugged to the top, lingered a breath-holding moment, then plunged down, careening on the edge of three horseshoe curves before braking to a stop. I'd always loved roller coasters, but that day would be the last time I rode one.

Our turn came. While the seat we sat in climbed higher and higher, so did I, the mescaline a master puppeteer with my body and mind. The car made its first vertiginous drop, whipped around the curves, speeding down to the big valley at the end.

Joe and I clutched each other, laughing so hard I was afraid I'd pee my pants. I couldn't tell which arm was his and which was mine but then it seemed we were going way too fast.

I screamed along with the others as we flew past the exit.

I heard a young voice shout, "The brakes are out!"

Unchecked, the cars climbed again, this time whipping us around even faster. Flying past the exit a second time, Joe and I both white-knuckled the bar that held us in. The wooden rails groaned, they moaned, people behind and in front of us echoed our cries for help. Flung around one more time, we pulled with all our strength on the bar as though it had the power to stop us. After this, the third round, the emergency brakes activated, grinding the cars to a whiplashing stop. Joe and I both needed assistance to get out, our legs too wobbly and weak beneath us.

Accelerated by the adrenaline rush, I felt the mescaline flushing through my system. We stumbled down the boardwalk's wide wooden steps to collapse flat on the sand, Joe first next to me, then on top. He kissed me, our first kiss, his lips dry, soft and tentative, and that was the moment I fell in love. Or was it lust? At that age it never occurred to me that there might be a difference.

After that day Joe and I were rarely apart, but since I wasn't a member, he wanted to keep our relationship a secret from his Revolutionary Union comrades. Apparently close personal liaisons were discouraged with people outside the organization. I wasn't happy about that, but to deflect the possibility of rejection, I agreed.

9

RADICALIZED

In October 1969, hundreds of thousands of people took part in a nation-wide strike to end the Vietnam War. A month later, in Washington D.C., more than 250,000 showed up to protest, more than 100,000 in Boston. People were moving.

Joe and I were spending more time together. We were still a little shy with each other; he was my first real boyfriend and, more than likely, I was his first girlfriend. We often worked as a team, running leaflets off on the mimeograph machine and handing them out during lunch hour on campus. I'll always associate the smell of ink with him.

I was beginning to understand that love might not be enough of an answer to the many disparities in the world, not when we were dealing with a government that cared only for protecting the rich and entitled. As I learned more about the Revolutionary Union, and its possibilities for the future, the more attractive it was.

I began attending meetings of RAM (Radical Action Movement), the RU's anti-war front group on campus. One night we hosted a poster-making party in anticipation of a protest against corporate recruiters from the top defense contractors—Lockheed, General Electric, Standard Oil, and nearly fifty others—who were invited by the school to interview students about to graduate.

I laughed at a friend who was writing all the war profiteer's crimes in letters so small I could barely see them.

"Good idea, but nobody will be able to read them, Susan," I said. "Maybe make multiple signs, break it up."

She sat back on her haunches and laughed with me. "Okay, your idea, you've got to help me!"

Foregoing words, she drew a picture of General Electric's machine gun while I drew the helicopter ubiquitous in the war, a Lockheed C5-Galaxy. I framed both within circles with a black line crossed on the diagonal. We made another sign for Standard Oil's rape of Vietnam's oil fields, and Dow Chemical's destructive napalm and Agent Orange.

There were about a dozen of us in the room and I thrived in the camaraderie as we prepared for the first campus protest I would participate in.

On the day the recruiters arrived, more than a hundred students led by RAM surged up the outside stairs of the student center, chanting "Pigs off campus! Smash Imperialism!"

Stopped at the top by campus security backed up by the city police, we were ordered to disperse. In our meetings, we discussed for hours whether or not RAM should be on the offensive. Ultimately it was decided that this would be a nonviolent event. But stuck on the stairs, it was difficult to comply when the demonstrators ahead of me were jumped by cops and beaten with nightsticks. In the melee, I ducked my head and squirmed my way down to join the crowd of chanting students gathered on the quad below. Incited by the cacophony, I yelled to the point of hoarseness.

The rush that followed reinforced my confidence that WE were right and THEY were wrong. Joe and I had already been talking about my joining the Revolutionary Union and that night I told him I was ready.

He went to leadership, both to disclose our relationship and to tell them of my desire to join. I eagerly waited for him in the student center, nursing a cup of coffee and a cigarette.

"What did they say?" I asked as soon as he walked in.

"First they scolded me for engaging in a personal relationship without prior permission, but then tentative approval was given with the caveat I coach you on the ideology of Mao Tse-Tung and Marxist-Leninism." Before sitting down, he leaned down and kissed my forehead. So sweet, I thought.

I was thrilled and didn't think to question whether I was doing this for myself or to be with Joe, but in retrospect I think they were pretty evenly weighed. Mostly I was relieved to find what I believed to be straightforward solutions to the complicated challenges of capitalist exploitation.

Before the second semester, over the winter break, I moved from the dorm into a house nearby with other left-leaning students. The clapboard house, located in the student ghetto outside of campus, had two bedrooms and a screened-in porch in the back that became my room. I was the fifth in a group of third-year students who continued to live there through the school year until summer.

I knew my mother wouldn't be happy so I waited until I settled in to call her.

"Mom, I moved. I'm renting a room, it's much less than the dorms, and I hated it there." I tried for a nonchalant tone, but in truth, I was nervous. My parents were still paying my rent.

"What are you thinking, Jody? You agreed to stay in campus housing for the first two years at least!" Her voice ratcheted to a yell. Instinctively I took a step back, knowing that if I were in front of her, her fisted arm would be swinging.

I had forgotten that promise but that the cost was considerably less won her over.

When I first went away to college, my parents and I agreed that I would call them every Sunday night at seven p.m. It was harder to do that once away from the dorm. Our house didn't yet have a phone, but I tried hard to get to nearest telephone booth two blocks away to maintain the connection. Mostly my mom would talk, catching me up on family and neighborhood gossip, boring me silly. I kept my side of the conversation short, telling her about classes and that I met a guy I liked, but nothing that hinted of the political direction I was going in.

Joe's and my study sessions took place in the common room at the student union. Spread out on the table were mimeographed sheets of the RU position papers and copies of speeches from China's party members translated to English. He tutored me in a crash course of Mao's *Red Book*, a small plastic edition filled with the Chairman's quotes divided into chapters like Classes and Class Struggle, The Mass Line, Education and The Training of Troops, Serving the People, and Correcting Mistaken Ideas. The language and vocabulary was as foreign to me as Chinese but, always diligent, I filled a notebook of school-lined paper, the margins further annotated with questions like: Are we already at war? What is the military strategy of peoples' war? Who are the "people?" Why does it have to be violent? Where does love come in? Joe's nearly illegible scribbles in response scrawled sideways across the page.

At our seventh or eighth meeting he handed me a sheet of paper that listed the four basic tenets of the Revolutionary Union: the necessity of a disciplined Communist party; the necessity of armed struggle; the necessity of a dictatorship of the proletariat; and the leading role the proletariat must play, both practically and ideologically, in the revolutionary movement.

"A disciplined party makes sense, but why is armed struggle necessary?"

"What do you think, Jody, that the ruling class will just hand over the reins to us? They'll have guns, we have to as well." He opened the *Red Book* to a page much underlined and read aloud:

> *Revolutions and revolutionary wars are inevitable in class society, and without them it is impossible to accomplish any leap in social development and to overthrow the reactionary ruling classes and therefore impossible for the people to win political power. Every Communist must grasp the truth: political power grows out of the barrel of a gun.*

"I don't like guns." I heard too late how much I sounded like a petulant child. Ready to be accused of having a petit-bourgeois mindset, instead Joe opened the little *Red Book* to another page.

> *As far as our own desire is concerned, we do not want to fight even for a single day. However, if circumstances force us to fight, we can fight to the finish.*

"Have you ever fired a gun?" he asked.

"No, not unless you count target shooting in the arcade."

Joe's look was censuring, much like any teacher with a recalcitrant student.

"This is absolutely confidential but you should know that the RU has a military arm with an arsenal. Rule by the working class can't be achieved without armed revolution and we all are expected to be skilled shooters. Every comrade must be ready to fight with weapons and each and every comrade must possess basic firearms, Jody. If you don't think you can do that, you should walk away now."

He lit a cigarette, so casual, then handed it to me to light mine off it.

I might have nodded; I only know that I did not question further. The possibility of using a gun and that I might one day take a life or be killed myself did not penetrate my consciousness, even as I understood that the ruling class would not give up their power voluntarily. My uneasiness was subsumed by the belief that the RU's formula for making the world an equitable place could be realized. I imagined a rosy future under their leadership, one inclusive of all regardless of the color of their skin, their gender, or how much money they had.

Joe looked at his watch. "I have a class in fifteen minutes. Let's move on. Next are the rules of discipline," he said, reading from a RU document.

The individual is subordinate to the organization; the minority is subordinate to the majority; the lower level is subordinate to the higher level; the entire membership is subordinate to the central committee.

According to that mandate, all personal relationships were valid only if they served the revolution. Art for art's sake, music for music's sake, intimacy with those who weren't comrades—all were considered anti-revolutionary. There should be no separation between a person's ideology and his or her being; nothing should take precedence over political practice.

I was confused and at a loss, especially when it came to my close friendships in Los Angeles. My longtime girlfriends were already worried by the singular path I had taken, and sent me letters expressing concerns that in my newborn zealotry I was letting my studies go. These friendships did not serve the masses, only me, but could I give them up? This dichotomy would remain at the core of the many ways I would eventually fail to be the good communist I aspired to.

* * *

Early in February 1970, campuses across the nation mobilized in marches and demonstrations against the war. The furor intensified after Nixon announced his intent to mine North Vietnam's main harbor to prevent the flow of arms to Ho Chi Minh's North Vietnamese Army. This was a radical move, neither approved by Congress nor the Secretary of Defense.

A few of us from RAM drove up to Berkeley to join a protest demonstration. It was a cold day—rain threatened. We joined thousands in front of Sproul Hall where, in 1964, the Free Speech Movement was born. Then, Mario Savio gave a rousing argument against the university's attempts to suppress civil rights activists on campus. I had a sense of the historical significance of the place, of those brave radical men and women who came before me. On that day more than a dozen spoke—members of the Black Panthers, SDS, RU, SNCC, and Brown Berets. The plan was to walk a peaceful mile to rally again in People's Park, but the vanguard running first were already smashing windows.

Several storeowners stood on the sidewalk urging them away from their stores, their fingers held up in a V for peace. The owner of Cody's Bookstore, popular with the left, stood outside holding a handmade sign reading "Peace, not violence!" The crowd plundered on, frenzied in their anger and rage against the government's betrayal of the will of the majority of Americans. A Gallup poll revealed that 56 percent of voters favored withdrawing our troops, as opposed to 37 percent the year before, but Nixon had no regard for popular opinion.

Although I wasn't trashing the glass fronts myself, every window shattering thrilled me as another strike against the enemy. The cops, close on our heels, shot wooden bullets into the crowd. The air strangled with lobbed canisters of mustard gas. I ducked two rocks thrown back by people ahead of me. My asthma flared from both running and the gas, forcing me into a doorway set back from the street as labored breathing sank me to my knees.

It took several puffs from my asthma inhaler before my breathing normalized. Police ran by holding bulletproof shields, using their clubs to strike anybody within reach. Terrified to be seen and routed out, the weak one culled from the herd, I pressed as flat as possible against the locked front door of a printing business. Rain drizzled, not soaking, not yet.

Once most of the cops and marchers passed, I stumbled from my hiding place to make my way back to the university, hoping the friends I'd driven up with would find me there. The campus, swathed in the haze of tear gas, was quiet. I sat on the wide steps of Sproul Hall taking protection under the overhang, leaning against one of the Corinthian columns, and looked out at the late winter flowers budding among the double row of pollarded London Plane trees. Their gnarly branches protruded from rough-hewn trunks like beseeching arms on an Alberto Giacometti sculpture. The trees stood as impassive witnesses to the generations of students before and for those still to come, evoking dark thoughts of how transient my time on the planet was. I forced myself up to standing, propelling myself to action. There was no room for existential anxiety in the life of a revolutionary. I paced up and down the promenade, alternately smoking a cigarette and puffing on the inhaler, until my friends arrived, faces flushed, to gather me up just as the rain backed off.

Soon after the second semester started, Joe deemed me familiar enough with Maoist ideology to meet with Barry Greenberg, the regional RU chairman. We sat in his living room on a cat-clawed sofa, our cups of coffee sitting atop newspapers spread across a low table. He quizzed me on theory, and always good at tests, I was able to answer his questions about the contributions necessary to be a good Communist. Satisfied, he anointed me a member of the student collective.

According to my transcripts, I was still going to class—modern dance, elementary Spanish, Western culture and society, and biology, but I barely recall attending. I preferred the world where I solidly belonged, where the so-called "bad" behavior of my youth was an asset to be utilized, not a problem to be solved.

My first meeting with the student collective was held in an apartment belonging to Charles, the collective chairman. He was an early member of the RU who came from Palo Alto to San Jose with Barry Greenberg, his wife Marianne, and Joe. About ten people crowded in, several women, but mostly men. We sat on the floor of his sparsely furnished living room in a cloud of cigarette smoke. The walls and carpet were beige; it looked like any other student apartment. Most of us were freshmen although a few were sophomores. A discussion ensued about the chapter from the *Red Book* they had assigned themselves to read, but I only remember how I felt, nothing that was actually said. Almost tongue-tied with shyness, I sat back as item after item was ticked off a printed agenda.

A report from the treasury committee was passed around and reviewed:

> It is the responsibility of all members to contribute money to the organization. Further, all comrades should remember to turn in their income tax refunds. Dues are $5 per person each month, or at least one third of monthly income. One third of this goes for local expenses, two thirds to central. More is needed. I recommend untapped resources, including savings accounts, stocks, and trust funds. The local executive committee has formulated the following guidelines, under Mao's general principles of frugality and plain living. The model monthly budget for one person living with others is $125 for rent, food, utilities, and car expenses. Every comrade should stop to think before they eat out that the money they spend could be better used by the organization.

Having no money other than the $100 sent me monthly by my parents, I didn't give much thought to this announcement.

When volunteers were requested to staff the literature table set up outside the student union, my hand shot up—that I could do. One of the women offered to talk me through what it would entail. Flushed with a sense of validity, I went home that night aglow with the connections made.

I found it both interesting and educational sitting at the RU table. Displayed were Mao's *Red Books*, the *Communist Manifesto* by Karl Marx and Friedrich Engels, *Das Kapital* by Karl Marx, and other books and pamphlets authored by Vladimir Lenin and Chinese luminaries. Dozens of people walked by each day, most without looking over but a few stopped and when they did the conversations gave me an opportunity to shine. As enthusiastic as any new convert, I spoke in the warmest of tones about the promises of Communism, urging them to picture a day when the tools of manufacture were owned by the workers rather than bosses exploiting their labor. At the time, it all made sense to me. I saw no other path to a world without exploitation and oppression.

Most of the student collective members participated actively in R.A.V.E. (Radical Audio Visual Experiment), a broad-based anti-war coalition that RAM was a part of. RAVE sought to educate on campus by showing radical movies like *The Battle of Algiers, On the Waterfront,* and *The Birth of a Nation* in the student union. Rousing anti-war speeches followed, given by Joe and other comrades.

My days filled quickly. I wrote and edited leaflets and pamphlets with diatribes against the military-industrial complex and in support of Ho Chi Minh's North Vietnamese army, helped organize student demonstrations, and circulated petitions to end the college's association with the ROTC (Reserve Officer Training Corp.).

I enjoyed working with single-minded purpose within the small community of my comrades, all as committed as I was. Most of us were new to this level of the student movement and friendships formed easily. I became closest with two women, Pamela and Meg, with whom I would eventually live. I thrived in the warmth of our camaraderie. Of the two, I was closest to Pamela, though Meg and I had more in common—both from Los Angeles and both our fathers were self-employed businessmen. Pamela and I couldn't have been more opposite. From a close-knit Irish Catholic working-class family, she was studying to be a nurse. She was small, almost birdlike with delicate bones, maybe 5'2". Still, there was a connection when we first met that only deepened once we were comrades in the Revolutionary Union.

The greatest boon—I found a family with whom I fit, a family who didn't care whether my hair was straight or curly, or teased me for laughing too loudly. Nobody commented on my height, nobody looked askance at my teeth or feet. For the first time I was forging my own way, definitively leaving behind my parents' expectations and my erratic self-destructive past.

I was busy, we all were. There was a war to stop and a government to overthrow.

During my second semester, on April 30, 1970, two months after the march in Berkeley, President Nixon covertly sent American military troops into Cambodia where they joined forces with the allied South Vietnamese troops called ARVN. Their mission was to disrupt supply lines, believing it necessary to defeat what they called the "domino effect" of spreading Communism beyond North Vietnamese borders. Our San Jose State anti-war coalition swelled with professors along with thousands of students as we joined campuses across the country in a general strike. We protested not only the war but also the severe reactive police tactics in quelling dissent.

By early May, more than three million students and faculty walked out of campuses across the country, shutting them down with demonstrations both violent and peaceful. Classes were cancelled; teach-ins prevailed, led by radical professors. At Kent State in Ohio, a peaceful demonstration against the invasion of Cambodia and continued war in Vietnam turned violent when students set fire to an armory used by the ROTC. The governor called in the National Guard, who shot more than sixty-seven rounds in thirteen seconds against unarmed students. Four were killed; nine wounded. An iconic photo from that day of a girl kneeling next to a boy who was shot, arms out-flung, mouth open as if screaming, forehead clenched as though in shock, circulated through the national press. One of those disabled became paralyzed. Two of the students killed or maimed were not even part of the protests but caught in the crossfire while they were walking between classes. This barbaric violence further polarized Americans, generating even more activists against the war.

Two weeks later, during a protest at the predominately Black Jackson State College in Mississippi, the police fired into the crowd, killing two students and wounding twelve others. At colleges in Seattle and Maryland, students vandalized the Air Force ROTC classrooms. Demonstrators at the University of Connecticut were arrested after blocking an intersection in the city's downtown. At least thirty ROTC buildings were burned down or bombed on colleges throughout the country while National Guard units mobilized on twenty-one campuses in sixteen states.

More than 100,000 demonstrated in Washington D.C. Ray Price, Nixon's key speechwriter during that time, was quoted as saying: "The city was an armed camp. Mobs were smashing windows, slashing tires, dragging parked cars into intersections, throwing bedsprings off overpasses into the traffic below. That's not student protest, that's civil war." Absolutely. It was a national uprising, the like of which had never been seen in the United States. President Nixon had the gall to misinform the public by labeling the protesters "pawns of foreign communists."

In September the same year, the president initiated "Operation Tailwind," another secret invasion by American troops, this time in southeast Laos. Its intention to distract the National Liberation Front (South Vietnamese soldiers supporting the North) fighting American troops in Vietnam was carried out by spraying toxic nerve gas. After an investigation, a congressional investigation found no fault by the US government. We were not surprised.

All these incidents fueled my certainty that I was on the side of justice, doing necessary work against the evil empire.

10
COMMITTED

A bomb constructed by the Weathermen intended for a military gathering in New Jersey accidentally exploded in the subbasement of a townhouse in Greenwich Village. The burning building collapsed, killing three members of the group. A few months later, two homemade bombs made from an electric blasting cap, an alarm clock, a battery, and a plastic bag filled with gasoline exploded under the steps of a ROTC building in Chicago and at the North Carolina police headquarters. Ten more bombs were set off by the Weathermen in various government buildings and corporate sites, including the Presidio in San Francisco, a Long Island courthouse, a bank in New York, and a Capitol building in D.C. These actions were roundly condemned by the Revolutionary Union, concerned that the violence would alienate the working class.

During that time I was busy working the mimeograph machine, selling RAM's newspaper, *Maverick*, on campus and on the streets, and attending planning meetings, but had no time alone with Joe. Indeed, since our date in Santa Cruz, our time together other than occasional sleepovers were always with other people. I wanted more. There were times I wanted to drag him away, but the comrade to whom I confided this reminded me that the work we were doing was more important. I accepted that—what else could I do? It's what I signed up for.

The student collective met five to six times a week to discuss strategy and tactics that would give us influence over the protest movement. They were highly charged, each of us eager to share our thoughts. At least once a week we analyzed sections of the *Red Book,* struggling to translate its meaning into our everyday practice.

On campus, I gained a reputation as a persuasive speaker, the one handed the bullhorn when speeches were over, and it was time to move the crowd. My body and voice commanded and I was one of the few in my collective good at firing up action. For the first time I was proud of being big and loud, unchecked by the constraints of self-loathing. It felt good to identify the enemy and expose them for the tyrants they were. I had a sense of belonging to something bigger, being on the inside of a community of my own making, on my own terms.

I have a photograph of me standing on a stage outside the student union, a microphone to my mouth. It must have been cold—I was wearing the brown corduroy coat that I kept until threadbare. My face blemished with acne, hair in a half-ponytail, I look serious, not a trace of a smile at the moment the camera shutter clicked, but that belied how much the call and response thrilled me.

What do we want?
PEACE!
When do we want it?
NOW!

In San Jose, the Revolutionary Union became the core of all actions. More people joined and I loved seeing our numbers swell. The workers and community collectives were also growing and the time was ripe to fan the flames for revolution, to make it clear how responsible the military-industrial complex's drive for profits was steering the war and suppressing civil rights. Our mimeograph machine limped day and night, spitting out leaflets calling for a proletariat uprising. These were passed out on the streets and outside factory parking lots as their workers drove into work. Our fingers were always ink-stained. There were other communist organizations on campus—the Progressive Labor Party and Socialist Workers Party—but our ideologies differed. They disdained us and we disdained them. Occasionally fistfights would break out between their members and ours. Of course, we were the only ones with the correct point of view, with the strategies to stage and win the revolution.

The general strike ended three weeks later as students returned to class to take finals, but my collective, thinking me more valuable as a full-time activist on campus, asked me not to return. I had no problem with that. Now was the time to capitalize on the gains made by the RU as leaders in the anti-war movement. I was elated by the notice and honored by the sense of value and worth they placed on me. Unfortunately, my precipitous withdrawal caused my teachers to give me incompletes, which later reverted to fails. I gave the grades little thought then, although in the future in a different place and a different time, this decision would come back to make trouble when six years later I wanted to return to college.

Although my parents knew I was active in the general strike, I couldn't tell them I had dropped out—they were still sending me money for food and rent.

Still, my father suspected something was up and sent me a short letter:

With what is happening on campuses these days, our thoughts are much with you. I feel strongly against any escalation of a pointless war, just exactly as you do. However, I do hope in the emotional rush of events you can stand back and observe yourself dispassionately if you are inclined to get caught up in violent action. I think it is very right to march and to speak out —to write—to act, but only in a non-violent framework as your revered Dr. King advocates. I know that you have always had a singular-single-mindedness in what you do—to throw yourself whole-heartedly into the thing that preoccupies you, but please don't lose your cool.

I was touched by his care and moved to respond:

I'm all right—please rest easy when thoughts turn to me—I am not responding negatively against the present system whose price of freedom is so high, but positively toward the evolution of man that will raise us all—not in anger but in a fierce love that won't allow me to pacify myself within my own family.

What I couldn't admit even to myself was that my dad was right about my single-mindedness and impulsivity, that indeed I had jumped in with both feet and all my heart. But that was me —how could I do otherwise?

In the RU's eagerness to emulate working-class families, leadership decided that all couples dating should move in together.

This wasn't difficult for me. By then I was sure of my love for Joe and felt he might love me. But how our living together would make a difference to those we were trying to recruit was never clear to me and I see now how foolish their thinking was—how much it revealed an elitist observation of the lifestyle habits of the proletariat. In the 1970s, I doubt that anybody who might care about the revolution would care less about Joe's and my living situation. Still, as always, I did what I was told.

We moved together to a bedroom in the house that I was already sharing with other RU comrades. On the day that he brought two rifles to stow under our bed, he didn't ask if I was okay with that. Though if he had, I probably wouldn't have objected. If I didn't accept it, I was disavowing the coming revolution, and was nowhere close to taking that stance. But once in our bed, Joe resisted any intimacy. Gone was the excitement and passion of our early courtship. I wasn't sure what he wanted from me, what he was thinking, whether he was being dutiful or really wanted to share a bed and home with me. Was I was too big? Too loud? Something I did must have alienated him. However subliminal, I was still in the grip of self-loathing, and believed it was my fault when he began sleeping on the far side of the double mattress, a pillow covering his face.

Despite my many advances, we made love hardly at all in the months we lived together, and then usually after Joe was drinking. I'd never been in bed with a man who didn't want sex and I didn't know if he was rejecting me or holding back for reasons of his own. I lay awake night after night, wondering what I'd done to diminish Joe's affection. Gifted at speechmaking, he was virtually tongue-tied when it came to emotions and I was no better. My weak attempts to talk to him were shot down with sharp criticism of my selfishness. He was overcome with work—there were pamphlets to write, speeches to give. Did I put my needs above the revolution? he asked. I backed off. It was too easy to believe myself undeserving of love. Confused, I didn't know how much longer I could live with a boy who longer seemed to care for me.

Joe thumbtacked a poster of Joseph Stalin, considered a hero by Maoists, on the wall above our pillows. I knew only a little about Stalin's massive campaigns of repression and genocide against the Jewish population in Russia, and found it hard to believe that the anti-Semitic dictator was embraced by Chairman Mao. My objections were more emotional than knowledgeable so I kept my mouth shut. In my compartmentalized way, I decided not to think about this, although I made sure to take it down for my parents' brief visits.

Almost summer, on a blue-skied afternoon, I was driving a friend's car down First Street, a wide boulevard in downtown San Jose, when a dreadlocked steel-grey dog trying to cross caused drivers to brake and swerve and lean on their horns. I didn't hesitate, didn't even take a breath to consider, but pulled up the emergency brake lever and jumped out. Frantic, her dilated pupils hiding white, the dog skittered this way and that, always circling back to the spot I first saw her. Now I was getting honked and screamed at, but I was intent on getting that dog to safety and knew I had to approach her slowly so not to startle her into running farther away. She jumped away from my first and second reach, but for the third, I pretty much dropped my body on hers, wrestling her down until I had a good enough hold to tuck her like a football under my arm. Back in the car, the dog on my lap crushed against the steering wheel, I jammed the clutch, released the brake, and tore away in first gear until I could get curbside and move her over.

"So who are you?" I asked. She smelled like fermenting

trash, her feet were mud-caked. "Phew! Have you ever had a bath?"

Cowering in the passenger seat, her eyes darted, ears laid back, fur bristled. No collar, no way to ID her if indeed she ever had belonged to anybody. I thought she might be two, maybe three years old. Her teats were swollen; she must have recently given birth.

"Listen, I don't know what I'm going to do with you, but there's about to be a meeting in my house and you're going to have to come with me."

Intent on getting home on time, I didn't think any further into the future.

When I walked in late, everybody wondered about the dank piece of crusty fur I brought with me. Did I even think about keeping her? I don't recall thinking otherwise.

After everybody left, I cut the furry mats off her as best I could and gave her a bath in our farm-sized kitchen sink. She fit handily in the basin, likely not weighing more than twenty pounds, more bones than fat. I dumped pot after pot of water over her, and as the dirt puddled around her feet, she emerged no longer grey, but shades of black with random white markings. I named her Buffy, for Buffy St. Marie, a protest singer I admired.

Within a minute, we were a love-match, and that was how we would remain for eight more years. She was my steadfast companion, moving with me to two more cities, until I lost her to stomach cancer in 1978.

11

DIVIDED

About two months after the night of the failed shoot-out, on August 15, 1970, Maria Dolores Sanchez, a United Farm Workers organizer that I met at an anti-war march the week before, called me early in the morning. By then I had been a member of the Revolutionary Union for close to a year. She was hoping I could bring reinforcements to join the U.F.W. picket lines in Salinas, an hour south of San Jose. That morning, seven thousand lettuce pickers went out on strike against the Teamsters and growers who refused to recognize their newly formed union. She asked me to bring as many as I could round up. In response to my calls, five carloads of local activists soon gathered outside my house. Gerry passed around steaming cups of coffee and donuts that he and his carload picked up from the Winchell's around the corner.

The sun was slow to show itself through the thinning marine layer, though it would burn through soon enough. I waited in the driver's seat of my roommate's Volkswagen that I promised to return in time for her evening shift at the phone company. Two comrades, Ken and Pamela, sat in back, while Miles (the high schooler) was next to me in front. When all was ready, I pumped the sticky clutch into first gear, then let the engine sputter when I saw Miles open the glove compartment and place a handgun, wrapped in a white T-shirt, under a stack of maps and box of Kleenex.

"Are you kidding? Get that out of here!"

Other cars were idling, waiting for me to take the lead. A horn honked, then another.

"Jesus Christ, Miles! We're going to support the farmers, not start a war!"

Charles came to my window. "What's the problem?" he asked, drumming his fingers on the roof.

"Miles's got a gun! It's in the glove compartment!"

"No big deal. Just leave it there, Miles, okay? C'mon, Jody, let's get going." He thumped the roof of my car before walking back to his.

"Don't worry, Jody. You always worry." Miles's smile was both endearing and arrogant. He quoted Mao Tse-Tung: *Political power grows out of the barrel of a gun.*

I pulled out, stripping the gears as I shifted into first.

Miles laughed. "Want me to drive?"

I found Maria Dolores in a dirt parking lot already filled with road-worn trucks and cars. She asked me to accompany her to the farm across the road, while my friends were directed to a bus that would take them to more distant fields.

Across the two-lane highway, Maria Dolores and I linked into a tangled chain of migrant and local farm workers who were blocking access to the largest corporate-owned lettuce field in Salinas. Red flags silk-screened with the stylized black eagle of Cesar Chavez's United Farm Workers Union hung limp from hand-held poles in the blooming oppressive heat. Maria Dolores was dressed comfortably in the *campesino* garb of white cotton pants, a hand-embroidered *huichol* top, and leather *huaraches*. I wished I had thought to bring sunglasses and a hat.

We circled the several truckloads of scabs brought in by the grower's foremen. Dry dirt roiled in the wake of our footsteps, dirtying the air already polluted by exhaust fumes from the trucks. Coffee-colored men and women stood corralled on the railed flatbeds, most of them sullen and staring at their feet, a few tall and belligerent. If not for hunger, they likely would rather be anywhere but there.

Holding hands, Maria Dolores and I walked behind an old man wearing much-laundered cotton pajama pants without a shirt. Scarred pockmarks pitted his back and chest. Exhilarated, I took mental photographs of those walking with us: whole families, big sisters and brothers carrying the youngest, the stooped elderly, babies strapped onto their mother's chest with wide strips of cloth, little girls and boys on the side chasing each other, some kicking a soccer ball, others competing in a game of stickball. Sweating bottles of soda, free for the taking, sat on blankets shaded by brightly striped beach umbrellas where the youngest and oldest rested.

An old man hanging off the truck rails gave the grandfather the finger, yelling to him, "Mario Vasquez! *Chinga tu madre!*" I thought perhaps they had once been friends, but now it was scab vs. striker.

The man ahead of me hawked a gob of phlegm into the road. His aged arms, ropy sinews of muscle bagged in creped skin, wildly gesticulated. Before the fight could escalate, a convoy of black and white vans raced up, barely braking before dozens of cops wearing riot gear swarmed out with rifles drawn.

The strikers' chants intensified, fists punched the air.

Huelga! Huelga! Huelga! Strike! Strike! Strike!

A police commander, squat and thickly muscled, racked and fired a shotgun over his head, the loud clap making me jump. He announced through a bullhorn that the strikers would be jailed if we didn't disperse. A few left—those with children and some of the elderly. The querulous grandfather was led away by a young girl I assumed was his granddaughter. I considered my roommate's car keys in my pocket and the promise I made to return the VW to her early, but what worried me the most was Miles's pistol in the glove compartment and what might happen if it was left on the field.

I vacillated about what to do, but my decision was made when Maria Dolores gripped my hand and pulled me to the ground beside her. I sat crossed-legged in the dirt amid a babble of Spanish too fast for me to translate in my head and tried to put my fears to rest.

The commander again ordered the strikers to leave. A few more did. He gave the order to arrest us, en masse. Right away, Maria Dolores was plucked from our circle, handcuffed and taken to the backseat of a patrol car. I stood up to protest, but the women on either side of me held me back, one in English telling me it was okay, I shouldn't worry, Maria Dolores would be all right.

Having grown up together, the rank-and-file policemen were taunted and teased by the local strikers. With jaws clenched below frowning mouths, the cops pulled up one person, then another. Most of the strikers went limp, forcing the cops to drag or carry them.

"Her?" the men asked their commander, pointing at me. Until then I hadn't realized that I was the only white girl there. His incoherent response became clear when I was hoisted into the air by two of his men, each at least five inches shorter than my six feet.

Their sweaty hands let me slip several times, just to grab a breast or grip between my legs. I writhed and kicked, but they held on until we reached a paddy wagon where I was tossed in with no more regard than for a sack of turnips. The women already inside helped me sit up, clucking with dismay. Once stabilized, I saw them all staring at me.

"We want to know, why are you here?" The young woman who asked had the round face and sloped forehead of her Mayan ancestors. Thick black hair tied back in a braid fell to her waist.

"I'm Jody, a friend, una amiga, of Maria Dolores's." That was enough to earn me warm smiles in welcome.

I counted—fifteen women including me filled the van. A Chicana officer not much older than my eighteen years crowded in and slammed the door. She cradled a rifle on her lap but rolled and slipped with the rest of us as the van sped away. Two narrow windows provided little light; the air was dank. Horribly susceptible to carsickness, within blocks spit thickened in the back of my throat. I kept swallowing, hoping desperately that I wouldn't throw up. When the van stopped only a few minutes later, the rear door was pulled open, sending those closest to the back tumbling out like dice onto the blacktop parking lot.

More paddy wagons drove up to the back of the Salinas jail. I looked closely and could see that all their passengers were from the same field as me. I knew then that the cars belonging to the strikers from farther fields would be gone by nightfall, leaving the blue Volkswagen exposed. Miles's gun was a knot in my stomach.

The young guard led us to the processing office where a harried-looking policewoman's shoulders visibly tightened as the room filled. After adding my name to a list, I parked myself on the floor between a desk and a filing cabinet, under a poster of President Nixon. There were close to seventy-five women to process, and I knew it would be a long time before my turn came. Without Maria Dolores, I felt timid among the women chattering in Spanish and was relieved when she finally emerged from an adjacent room, her eyes wincing in the fluorescent brightness.

She spoke to a few of the women then slid down the wall to sit beside me.

"Are you okay?" I whispered. "What happened?"

"Nothing really, just bullshit. I'm okay, just very tired, mi amiga, very tired. I think I could sleep for a week." She closed her eyes and rested her head on her knees.

I stood up to read the wanted posters pinned up on multiple bulletin boards. Men mostly, wanted for drugs, murder, and violent assaults. When I was young and in a post office with my mother, I always studied the pictures trying to memorize features in case one of them might cross my path, and the habit remained.

Finally the booking officer yelled "Forrester!" She had to extend the camera's tripod to its full height before directing me to place my feet on painted footsteps with little of the original outlines remaining. Face forward—flash. Turn to the side—flash. Fingers pressed onto an inkpad, then onto squares on a cardboard form. A routine I'd seen at least a hundred times on television, but this time it was me. I was equal parts fascinated and terrified.

"You'll see the judge in the morning," she said.

"Do you know what I'm being charged with?"

She looked at the paperwork. "Uh, let's see. Unlawful assembly, failure to disperse, and obstructing a peace officer."

Peace officers? More like pig officers, I thought.

"Morales!" she called.

I was directed to a telephone booth, allowed to make one

phone call. Ever mindful of the RU's need for secrecy and security, and given how likely it was the phones were tapped, I called a friend outside but close to the organization.

"Jack, it's Jody," I said when he answered on the third ring.

"Hey, I thought you were in Salinas." His voice, so normal and matter-of-fact, was in marked contrast to my agitation.

"Yeah, well, the line got busted. I'm calling from jail." I reached in my pocket for a cigarette before remembering they had been confiscated along with my keys and wallet, leaving only loose change.

"You're okay?" he asked.

"Okay enough. It's just that nobody knows where I am, so I need you to get in touch with Charles when he gets back. Especially remind him about my roommate's car. It's parked with the others. He'll know." I hung up quickly. His sympathetic tone aroused self-pity and tears, neither of which I dared indulge.

The women's jail was housed on the second floor of the station, and was as bleak as I would have imagined it—institutional green walls etched with profanities, stained yellowed linoleum, Venetian blinds hanging crooked from broken strings. Bare fluorescent tubes in the walkway cast a harsh and unforgiving light.

I joined the same women I had been packed with in the van, now packed into a cell with only two metal bunkbeds and less than four feet of floor space between them. There was a barred window high on the wall and a metal toilet seat over a dark hole, hand-woven shawls already lying beside it so the women could drape themselves when they sat down.

My cellmates were immigrant fieldworkers, many of whom had been brought into the United Farmworkers Union by Maria Dolores. The mood lifted once she joined us. Right away, she had them laughing so hard that tears spilled down sunbaked faces. She spoke too quickly for me to follow, but I understood from her gestures that she was telling them about an officer whose genitals peeked out of his shorts during her interrogation. I laughed with them, their gaiety my best assurance that everything would turn out all right. They had anticipated the police, Maria Dolores told me, and most of the women had made arrangements for their husbands and children to be cared for.

Over the next few hours, I became more comfortable using my high school Spanish, mostly nouns linked with present tense verbs. A young woman, telling me her name was Theresa, sat next to me on the cold floor sheltering an infant in a muslin wrap. He grasped my finger and I cooed. She asked if I would hold him while she used the toilet.

"*Si, gracias!*" Holding him aroused much emotion in me. He was so precious, so trusting. I tickled his belly with my nose, breathing in his scent of baby oil and cornstarch. The women watching me laughed. Some mocked my silly sounds; others caricatured my awkward pose. They teased, saying I could hold all of their children for as long as I wanted. When Theresa came back, the infant lunged for her breast.

With Maria Dolores translating, she asked if I had children.

I wondered if they knew how young I was or if it would matter. Theresa didn't look much older. "No, not yet."

Once she broke the formalities, other women rained questions on me.

"Where do you live?"

"Do you have a sweetheart? *Un novio?*"

"Where are your parents?"

I was astounded to learn that neither their daughters nor their sons would leave the family home until they married. They were scandalized that I didn't live with my parents, even when I told them I left only to go to college.

Many of them were old friends, having met early in their youth. I felt too big for the room—most of the women hovered around 5'2". My feet were like clown shoes next to theirs and I sat feeling more and more like a party crasher. The conversation shifted. They gossiped and argued about the strike while I tried to think of something to say that might bring the strike in context with my politics, but impaired by language, I could think of nothing.

Any gathering of people, especially when among those in the working class, was considered by the RU to be a golden opportunity to educate and guide, but the schism between the strikers' needs and our dogma troubled me. Now face-to-face, I couldn't see them picking up arms against their bosses, let alone the reigning government. What would be their motivation? Many left Mexico illegally in pursuit of a better life and wanted only to return to work protected by a strong union. My grandparents did the same when they escaped from anti-Semitism in Eastern Europe in the early 1900s, seeking only a living wage for their family, food on the table, and a house of their own. Success to them was a promise that their offspring might flourish. How could I, a young white college dropout, tell them they would be better off under the dictatorship of the proletariat? In jail, what did that even mean? Still, I was committed to following all the RU dictates and knew I should at least try to bring up the subject of capitalist oppression. I brooded on that but finally was too aware of my outsider status to summon up the nerve to speak out loud, even to Maria Dolores. It was a conundrum. I thought about Charles, imagining he would know what to say, but would he be right? Not for the first time I worried that I might be more enamored with the ideals and goals of Communism than with the actual ideology.

The rancid odor of a grease fire soon reached our cell and in a short while a guard came to say that we would have to do without dinner. Maria Dolores told her about Ana who was diabetic, and Theresa who must eat to nourish her son. They were allowed to leave but surprised us an hour later when they returned with baskets of food prepared by the family members of those arrested. The donut and coffee that was my morning meal had long been digested and I was hungry, my stomach growling so loud that the women closest to me giggled. Warm tortillas, roasted chicken, and ears of corn were dispersed among the cells, and for a while all that could be heard were the sounds of women crunching and swallowing. Finally sated, I longed only for a cigarette and a cup of coffee.

In the small cell, our bodies were the only pillows to rest upon. We filled the beds, two and three to a mattress. I settled on a top bunk squeezed next to Maria Dolores and laid my head on her lap while she rested hers on my back. I wanted so badly to tell her about the gun, to not be alone with its secret, but I knew she would not be sympathetic, and why should she be?

Lulled by the heat and cradled by soft murmurs and quiet laughter, my eyes soon shut but I couldn't fully relax. The RU's voice continued to haunt me, insisting on the leadership role that I should be assuming, while fear that Miles's gun would be discovered was multiplied by my worry for my roommate. If the car were impounded, the brunt of the charges would fall on her.

As the light outside greyed, only the low-wattage bulb over the toilet and the buzzing tubes in the hallway allayed the darkness. Hands on the schoolhouse clock mounted on the wall opposite me ticked by so slowly that at times I wondered if it had stopped. It was past nine, then ten, then eleven. Most of my cellmates fell asleep, snoring lightly, twitching in their dreams, the scent of unwashed bodies pervasive. I didn't know I had fallen asleep until indecipherable dreams merged into guitars strumming and men singing so insistently that I jolted awake, sliding Maria Dolores off my back. Something was happening outside.

    I climbed down to the floor and stood at the window on tiptoes. Below me was a swarm of sombrero crowns with wide brims. The men wearing them were illuminated by the candles they held and were singing *banderos*, love songs, to their wives, mothers, and daughters, singing from their hearts, from the heart of the community. In twos and threes, the women woke up, some comprehending more quickly than others what was happening. Several of the bigger women and I held one, then another, up to the window. They clapped their hands and cried, and I, too, began to cry, caught in the threads of sentiment woven by the music.

    Frankincense wafted in, sweetening the stale air. The musicians quieted to allow a priest to lead the Catholic Mass. Next to me heads bent over hands pressed together, rosary beads clicked. Although in contradiction to my godless ideology, I felt privileged to be a silent observer of their rituals. I couldn't help myself—the chorus of song and guitars touched me beyond the RU activist I had become and the atheist my parents raised me to be.

    After the men left, I lay down on the floor and this time fell into a deep sleep when a guard unlocked and opened the cell door. The sun was just filtering in. My eyes, crusty with sleep, peeled open.

    "Jody Forrester!" He pointed to me, assured of his choice.

    I was frightened and didn't want to leave alone.

    Maria Dolores, already awake, whispered, "*Sera fuerte*. Be strong." I hugged each woman whose name I'd come to know, feeling already the loss of our overnight intimacy.

    The guard led me downstairs to the same office where Maria Dolores had been taken the day before and locked me in without a word. The room was small with dark paneled walls and no windows, only a metal card table and a single chair on either side. It was the classic interrogation room of police dramas. Fretting and pacing, I was too restless to sit, just one thought circling: the gun, they must have found the gun. It seemed a very long time before the door swung open. I expected the commanding officer but instead it was the same guard who locked me in.

"You made bail. A lawyer is here for you," he said, his English broken with a Spanish accent. "Follow me."

A man in a navy blue suit and silk tie stood in the lobby. So dressed up, he looked like he'd taken the wrong exit off the freeway. He didn't introduce himself, only said that he was an attorney sent by a colleague to post the five hundred dollar bail bond.

Despite my fears about the VW, I strenuously objected. "We'll be arraigned soon. I should stay!"

"I'm following orders. The paperwork's already filled out and your bond's paid." His voice was tired. He must have been awakened very early to get there before eight.

The sergeant at the front desk handed me my things. Once outside, I lit a cigarette, but the lawyer in his new Mercedes asked me to put it out.

Sunlight diffused in the dusty ever-present haze in the Salinas valley. In clotted traffic outside the jail, women were pushing children in strollers, many carrying brightly colored straw shopping bags.

"Who sent you? Do you have a message for me?" I asked.

"Skip called me, reminding me that I owed him a favor." I recognized the name from the pool of attorneys supportive of the RU agenda. Charles must have called him.

"Nothing more?"

He shook his head, slowed at a stop sign, and then shot

through. The leather seats were slippery. I dug my toes into the plush floor mat.

We drove directly to the parking field. I could see immediately that the VW wasn't there, although I desperately continued to scan the few cars and trucks still parked.

"My car's gone!" I turned to him, expectant and hopeful. He must know something.

He shrugged. His lack of concern cautioned me to say no more.

A station wagon full of children drove up, the driver honking its horn. He leaned out the window, waving me over.

"That's it for me," the attorney said.

"Wait, what's happening? Who are they?"

He shook his head and reached over to open the passenger door. I was barely out when he took off, setting off a spray of dirt and stinging pebbles.

Five children were in the middle seat, all staring as I walked toward the car. A girl, maybe four years old, with pink and purple ribbons wound through her long braid, looked through her fingers at me, then ducked when I waved. The passenger door of the car was already open and I slipped in, trying not to cry in front of these people I didn't yet know.

In a jumble of Spanish and English, the driver introduced himself as Manuel, Maria Dolores's husband. He had the strong arms of a laborer and a reassuring sweetness to his voice. Seeing that I held a cigarette, he struck a match to light it. This simple courtesy calmed me.

"Are you Jody?" he asked, pronouncing the J as a Y as native Spanish speakers do.

"Yes. Thank you for picking me up." I could hear my voice, higher pitched than usual, as I struggled to hold back brimming tears. Manuel began driving, one hand on the wheel, the other stretched across the back of my seat.

"I left my car here yesterday, but it's gone." I could feel my face beseeching him.

"Sí, I know. I have it, now it's at my house." His wide smile revealed the great pleasure he took in my surprise and relief.

"How did, you know, how did you do it?" I asked. The tears spilled over—I could no longer contain them.

"It was easy, just a screwdriver. Your friend, the one with the stutter, phoned me last night. He explained the problem." Manuel didn't remember his name, but I knew it was Charles and sent a silent thank you to Jack for the message he must have passed on.

The children were giggling and curious. Little fingers touched my matted curls and one tried to comb through them.

"Maria called just a little while ago. She said the arraignment will be at nine and it's almost that now. I have to take you."

"Does she know I'm with you?" Still confused, I was trying to make sense out of what was happening.

"No, señorita. Your friend, he called again, just now, just as I was leaving for the court. He said that somebody would bail you out and I should find you here."

Manuel turned a corner and stopped to let me out in front of the courthouse next to the jail, saying he would see me soon. After a few wrong turns, my breathing tense, I found my group already lined up in front of the judge's bench awaiting his entrance. The other women picked up with us sat in wooden seats for their cases to be called. Maria Dolores turned and waved me over with frantic hand gestures.

"*Amiga, que pasa?* Your name, it was just called. Are you all right? Where did you go?"

The bailiff frowned. The judge was coming in; I could only squeeze her hand.

In less than ten minutes, a trial date was set and my cellmates released on their own recognizance. I was embarrassed by my privileged early release, though I realized nobody actually knew why I was called out of the cell earlier. I lost track of Maria Dolores and was not sure what to do next when Manuel, with his eye-crinkling smile, appeared out of the crowd to tell me that I should come home with them for breakfast.

"Then you can take your car." Had he been more familiar, I surely would have hugged him.

Maria Dolores was already in the front seat, twin toddlers on her lap. I crowded into the backseat with the children. The two daughters pushed their older brother away to sit next to me. Their mother settled the erupting quarrel with one stern look. We drove by deserted fields, the lettuce strike evidently still going on. At every entrance, U.F.W. representatives held up picket signs. Manuel honked the horn, I waved, the children cheered.

He soon pulled onto a bricked driveway leading to a low-slung ranch house, its cedar siding whitewashed below the roof's gray-brown shingles. Manuel shooed away several mongrels barking madly in greeting. Purple morning glory and pink bougainvillea straggled up the front of the house, anchored on nails set into the wood. Manny, their oldest (nine, I thought), pointed out a swing hanging from a heavily laden avocado tree. He told me he and his father had just finished making it for the younger kids. He spoke in accented English, very poised, very proud.

The living room was festive as though dressed up for a party. Paper flowers with floppy petals made of pink and blue tissue paper lay gathered in bunches behind the furniture and in every corner. Manny told me that they made them to sell. Finger paintings on school-issued newsprint were taped on brick walls. A zoo of piñatas that included Winnie the Pooh and Wile E. Coyote dangled from crossbeams next to multi-colored God's-eyes and flaccid balloons. Maria Dolores sighed when she saw the children's toys left scattered on the floor.

The house soon filled with spicy aromas. Manuel was in the kitchen, cooking *huevos rancheros*, sausage and breakfast potatoes, all smothered, Manny told me, in his dad's own tongue-burning salsa. When Manuel offered me a cup of coffee, I was so greedy for the hot caffeine that it was an effort not to just open my mouth and pour it in. We both lit cigarettes, his a hand roll, mine a Marlboro.

Fresh from the shower Maria Dolores joined us, the mess of toys on the floor already cleaned up. The beribboned girl, whispering to me that her name was Monica, stood leaning against my chair until I set her on my lap. This was the family life that I craved. Sitting at their table felt like coming home to a home I'd never known. Until Manuel spoke.

"So, your friend, he said there was a gun in your car." He sounded more amused than angry. "Yours?"

"Oh my god, no!" How could he even think that? But of course, he didn't know me.

"Then who?" His tongue curled to ferret out bits of tobacco from his front teeth.

"Just some stupid guy who thinks that every demonstration is a potential call for the revolution!" As soon as the words escaped my mouth, I wished I could take them back. RU members were expected to show a united front, our criticisms of each other aired only in meetings, but per usual, my mouth opened of its own accord.

"The *revolución*, I see." Manuel flicked his tongue out again to gather the stray pieces of tobacco. His lips still turned up, but whether it was a smirk or a smile, I wasn't sure. "And what *revolución* is that?"

Heat crept up my neck. Here was my opening, but I didn't know what to say, where to start. Monica clasped my hand as though she knew I needed reassuring. My mouth opened, my tongue twisted. Now that I had their attention, the words I hoped to say got stuck in my throat.

That was always my problem. I'm passionate about what I believe in and could argue against wrongs catalyzed by imperialism and capitalism but lacked the skill to present an in-depth argument about theory. I was never able to make the language my own. Dialectical materialism. Mass line. Class struggle. How the Maoism of an agrarian revolution pertains to the antagonistic struggle between labor and capital. The words stumbled. I took another deep breath.

"*Basta*, Manuel," Maria Dolores said. "Enough! This is a time to celebrate, not to talk politics!"

He laughed and the children laughed with him, eager to move the conversation back to themselves. I hated the relief I felt, knowing that once I returned home I would be expected to judge my performance and then be judged. What would be most important to my comrades was what I failed to do—I had not aligned the lettuce pickers' struggle with the proletariat revolution; I had not educated them about Mao Tse-Tung; I had made no contacts to follow up on. It would matter little that the women had liked me and that I had liked them. I could fairly be criticized for making myself more important than the Party line. I didn't know whether it was my immaturity or lack of confidence holding me back or the certainty that the farmworkers would have thought me ridiculous to think that I knew better what was best for them.

An hour later, satiated with food and family love, I followed Manuel outside to the VW parked behind their house. He stood back while I opened the glove compartment.

There it was, still wrapped in the shirt, oblivious of the worry it caused me. Manuel moved forward, took the gun out, and popped open the chamber. A bullet was housed there. He showed me, with a scolding look, that the safety latch was toggled open. Manuel ejected it, then pulled out the 8-bullet clip and put it in his pocket. I hoped he would take the gun too but didn't stop him when he returned it to the glove compartment. Embarrassed to blushing red, I couldn't look him in the eye, though I saw that the look he gave me was questioning and concerned.

I took the keys from my pocket, sat in the driver's seat, and started the car, driving around to the front where the children waited, their arms full of paper flowers.

"For you," Monica lisped.

They spread the floppy flowers on the back seat and put a few in the passenger seat, the pinks and blues a vibrant testimony to my value in their world. At that moment, I was glad I had been myself, with no agenda, without propaganda. I still remember their warmth and how much their inclusion meant to me. Their hugs cheered me as I left the house to drive north on the road I had taken south only the morning before. Soon enough I was on the highway, the windows open until the stink of rotting lettuce lying dormant in the fields got to be too much. I made sure to honk the horn each time I passed the strikers standing sentinel in front of empty fields.

Reluctantly, my thoughts spun forward. I still wished I could have taken some kind of a leadership role, but I was beginning to feel more confident in the reticence that held me back. Change, I think I had only just learned, depended on need, not dogma.

This was the first time it occurred to me that the Revolutionary Union might not have the right answers for everybody.

Once back in San Jose I found my collective so angry with Miles for bringing the gun and with Charles for allowing it that, to my relief, my short answers to their questions about the night before satisfied them.

"Contact has been made," they said. "Good for you, comrade!"

The charges against us were dropped; I never found out why. The grassroots United Farmworkers Union has since come to represent all field workers, not only those in the Central Valley but north into Oregon and southeast into Texas. That night was one my heart would always remember.

12

VIOLENT

On October 29, 1970, more than ten thousand demonstrators, including laid-off aerospace engineers and scientists, showed up outside the San Jose Civic Auditorium where Richard Nixon was speaking at a G.O.P. fundraiser. Inside I imagined all were cheering, while those of us outside waited for his exit to show our contempt and anger. When he finished, Nixon left the hall to the rear where his convoy, already surrounded by protesters chanting anti-war slogans, was parked. All was noise, nothing yet thrown, when the president, unanticipated by his security, climbed onto the hood of his limousine to flash two fingers in a peace sign to the crowd.

In his book, *The Memoirs of Richard Nixon*, he wrote, "I couldn't resist showing them how little respect I had to their juvenile and mindless ranting." At that point he was only one hundred and fifty feet from the flimsy barriers erected earlier by the police. Chunks of concrete from construction debris in the back of the parking lot started to fly. The secret service pulled him down, stuffing him into the back seat. The convoy started to move but stalled a moment later when the front car was hit with a rock producing a chain reaction crash of six vehicles. Numerous reports estimated that more than a thousand people threw eggs, rocks, and bottles.

I was standing just an arm's length away from Nixon's limousine when it stopped short. His scowling face and my wide-opened mouth reflected in the glass. Somebody handed me a fist-sized piece of concrete. Intimidated by fear, I first backed away but then adrenaline kicked in, ignited by scalding rage. My first strikes against his window were light but then a decision I was conscious of making pushed away my anxiety, providing the impetus to begin a full-scale offensive, pummeling and pounding the rock against the rear window. Cracks in the glass cobwebbed from each strike. I wasn't the only one. Demonstrators swarmed the car, some beating on windows, others on the roof. When the limousine lurched forward, I saw more than felt how bloody my hand was.

The next day President Nixon gave a speech in which he claimed: "The stoning at San Jose is an example of the viciousness of the lawless elements in our society." It was he who termed the event a "stoning," posturing himself as a sainted martyr. Given that the "lawless" elements included thousands of workers laid off as a result of his economic policies, he had a hell of a nerve.

Less than four years later, President Nixon would resign before he could be impeached for crimes related to the Republican-sponsored burglaries of the Democratic National Committee headquarters in D.C.'s Watergate office complex. Documents were stolen and wiretap devices installed. Nixon did everything he could to deny involvement but the intended cover-up led to indictments. I was disappointed he wasn't charged with war crimes, since that was truly what he was guilty of.

Years later, in my initial foray into the Internet for news

from that time, I found a picture in the *San Jose Mercury News* accompanying an article headlined the "Stoning of Nixon." Is that really me, the tall girl, her long dark hair held back by a kerchief, pounding a piece of concrete against the rear window of the president's limousine only inches away from Nixon's face? So angry, so aggressive, so bold, forever memorialized. I'm proud to claim myself as that well-intentioned young woman who truly believed evil could be defeated.

On the first of December that year, Nyguyen Cao Ky, the vice-president of South Vietnam, came to San Francisco to address a private club. With my RU collective, I was one of five thousand protestors clogging the street in front of the Fairmont Hotel where the meeting was to take place. Mounted and helmeted police from the SF Tactical Squad lined the block. Several police helicopters circled overhead. While Ky was still en route, the cops began herding us around the corner.

Somebody handed me a poster with a hand-drawn oinking pink pig wearing a police badge. I waved it in time to chants: *1-2-3-4—the NLF (National Liberation Front) is going to win!*

Rocks were thrown at cops on horseback. They moved in closer to cut their attackers from the crowd. Separated from my friends, I was looking for them when one of the riders moved in and kicked me in the stomach with the steel-capped toe of his boot, then pulled the sign away from me. Another cop jumped down from his horse, kneed me to the ground, striking my shoulder and chest with his nightstick. Two more grabbed me, one held my arms, the other my legs. I was fierce, writhing and twisting—no way they were going to take me. One finally trapped my hands behind my back. I heard the clank of handcuffs but still fought, making it impossible for the cop to hold my wrists together. My shoulders felt like they might pop from their sockets when, from nowhere, several longhaired boys in hippie garb dashed in, wrestled me away, and ran me over to the sidewalk. Before I could thank them, they dashed off again, likely to rescue others.

The San Francisco fog rolled in. It had been hovering most of the day but now swooped in with a vengeance. With visibility down to what was right in front of me, it was time to go. I was lucky that day—many of the protesters were charged with felonies, ranging from destruction of property to treason for acting against the U.S. government.

Later that night, when the collective met, I was the only one bruised. I showed off the oblong shape of a billy club visible on my thigh and a heel print on my belly, proof I was on the frontlines, proof that the pigs were out to get us. But I was concerned about the small businesses whose trashed windows were owned by people like my father who had no ties to the military-industrial enemies. I questioned that and others, also confused, agreed.

"Our actions are part of a bigger struggle, Jody, a guerilla action to further agitate in service of the revolution. There will always be collateral damage to those representatives of capitalism, however small." David, always the first one to throw a rock, offered this insight and in the moment it made sense. It was often hard for me to keep in mind our larger goals when some of the steps along the way were abhorrent to me.

After the meeting a few of us stayed behind, acting like the college-age teenagers we were—smoking weed, drinking cheap red wine. Terry stretched out on the couch, eyes closed, singing quietly about the labor activist, Joe Hill.

* * *

The week before Christmas, notice came from the regional executive committee in response to several members wanting to spend the holidays with their families:

> We are now in a period of intense ideological struggle and comrades should take this into account when planning time away. We ask all comrades to remain here over the holidays and use the time in meetings to review their participation over the past year, and decide on actions to take that will, in the future, amplify their commitment to the revolution.

I, however, was encouraged to go home. Those in leadership wanted me to get close to an organization called the Long March based in Los Angeles. Our politics were similar and it was hoped that they might want to join forces with the RU. For me it was a boon, an opportunity to catch up with old friends.

I flew into LAX several days before the holiday and was met by a solid wall of dry heat. Close to 85 degrees, even in Los Angeles it was too hot for December. My father was waiting by the curb for me. Although our relationship was more amiable by then, I was still a little guarded against him, a little nervous. He told me that my maternal grandmother wasn't well, and that we were stopping first at the small community hospital where she had been taken earlier that morning. Years of smoking had precipitated acute asthma and bronchitis. Not a large woman to begin with, in the bed that she lay on she looked like a wizened overripe potato. I cried to see her laboring for each breath.

I loved my grandmother—she had always been kind to me. Her hands were agitated, moving in a way that appeared as though she was knitting. I remembered her sitting with her sisters side by side on the couch in my mother's childhood bedroom. Three women making sweaters—one better at sleeves

—another at edging. Speaking Yiddish—soft cheeks—dear smiles. They loved me. I loved them.

It saddens me that my children have no visceral connection to their immigrant ancestors. My speech patterns, often thought odd, were the direct inheritance of spending my first seven years with native Yiddish speakers. These women ushered me toward my own aging years. How they laughed at themselves as they relied on my young eyes to find their dropped stitches, my young ears to translate what a waitress or shop woman was saying, and my strong arms to carry their purchases.

My Aunt Bea and I once drove to Dupar's Restaurant in Hollywood to pick up a loaf of our favorite date-nut bread. I stood on the black pavement of the parking lot waiting for her to haul herself out of the car and straighten her disheveled clothing. I was likely ten.

"In my mind," she said, "I can still leap out of the car, just like you, but my body has its own mind now. What can I do?" She shrugged. I loved her so much at that moment, both appreciating her confidence in me and sorry for the calamity of her aging body.

Now when I look in the mirror, I see her face and my grandmother's, and it makes me glad. Rather than rue my loosening skin and thinning hair, my resemblance to them makes me feel close to those who came before me.

The phone rang early Christmas morning. It was the hospital—my grandmother had passed. I stayed a long time in my adolescent bedroom, numb thoughts somersaulting between what I would wear that night to a Long March party to how very fucked up I must be. I felt nothing. I didn't know what to do, so I wandered outside and went to a neighbor's across the street just to tell them that my grandmother had died. I wondered what emotions might surface. Nothing. It didn't seem to affect me, although I know better now.

That night was the party and I went even though our extended family members were coming over for the first night of sitting *Shiva*, the weeklong mourning custom in the Jewish faith. I promised my mother I wouldn't be long and slunk off, aware of her annoyance. Guilt weighed heavily but not enough to keep me home. I needed to fulfill the obligation I had made to my collective given that that was the only reason I was permitted to go home. Another comrade in L.A. picked me up and we drove up to a brightly lit home of one of the Long March member's parents in an exclusive area in the Hollywood Hills. Outside and inside it looked like a Norman Rockwell Christmas. Colored lights on the eaves; a sixteen-foot tree bangled and tinseled; white people of all ages, most dressed in semi-formal green and red. Gallons of eggnog, at least a kilo of frosted cookies, and two trees' worth of mistletoe wreathing the mantle and pinned to the ceiling.

"So bourgeois," I said to my friend. She sneered in response.

The elderly hosts greeted us warmly, asked how I was, and since I could never answer that question casually in the way intended, I told them about my grandmother, taking note of their concern that I was there with them instead of with my family. Shame, more guilt. I changed my mind, wishing that I had stayed home, but my ride was already dancing and one of the cuter boys in the Long March was next to greet me. Soon we were dancing as well.

I didn't have to say much about the RU. It turned out that Long March leadership was already in discussion with our national headquarters. Instead, I danced and flirted and when the cute boy moved me under the mistletoe, his warm deep kiss weakened my knees. He pressed against me—I could feel he wanted me. In my loneliness and plummeting self-confidence since Joe abandoned me, the sense of gratitude aroused by this boy's desire allowed me to follow him to one of the back bedrooms.

But the sex was too quick and the cuddling I needed that night was aborted by his rolling off me to say, "Let's get back to the party!"

I followed brightly—with men, such a liar and pretender I could be.

13

UNRESOLVED

Produced by Dow Chemical, napalm was the most egregious weapon used by American and South Vietnamese soldiers. An incendiary mixture of a gelling agent and gasoline, the chemical mix burned at high temperatures and for a very long time, adhering tenaciously to its targets. Released by low flying planes, one firebomb could burn more than 2,500 yards, though far too often it was the napalm released by higher-flying planes that resulted in far more extensive damage to civilians.

Close to 400,000 tons of napalm bombs were dropped between 1963 and 1972, primarily in suspected areas of resistance. Called "liquid fire," the firebombs stuck to the skin for up to ten minutes, causing severe burns. It was most disastrous against those trenched in foxholes, bunkers, and ditches where it would concentrate. American generals deemed it their most effective war weapon.

A photograph seen worldwide became iconic of the damage wrought by the war. A nine-year-old girl running toward the camera, her clothes burned off, her mouth distorted in agony, her skin flapping, caused by a South Vietnamese attack on her village. Pictures of other children similarly scalded became quintessential images in the newspapers and on television, further mobilizing the American public to join the anti-war movement. These images incited crowds, putting the war in context of the evils of American capitalism and imperialism.

Although napalm caused greater damage to civilians, Agent Orange, a defoliant and herbicide, caused extensive damage to the fields and forests in South Vietnam, targeting areas where suspected sympathizers with the North congregated. Agent Orange was sprayed most intensively from 1961-71 and was widely known as part of the American Armed Forces herbicidal warfare program termed "Operation Ranch Hand."

More than six thousand missions flew over South Vietnam, destroying more than twelve percent of their agriculture. Four hundred thousand Vietnamese were killed by the pesticide's toxic effects and up to a million left disabled. What was unexpected was the destructive effect on American soldiers' health. All serving were exposed and the result became a public health nightmare. Birth defects, multiple cancers, and diabetes were only a few of the more severe illnesses suffered by our veterans. The U.S. government has since undertaken efforts to help those Americans affected but offered nothing to the hundreds of thousands of Vietnam citizens who suffered equally.

Ron Kovic, of Vietnam Veterans Against the War, led hunger strikes and spoke at the 1976 Democratic convention. Their membership grew exponentially from 1,500 to more than 20,000 when the Nixon administration ordered the invasion into Cambodia and after the Kent State shootings. A notable representative was another veteran, Senator John Kerry, who took their concerns to Congress but was summarily dismissed.

In 1971, the VVAW created the Winter Soldier Investigation to interview veterans, asking if they witnessed or participated in war crimes such as search and destroy missions, crop destruction, and POW mistreatment. The revelations were overwhelming and the results presented to the White House, but again the veterans were rebuffed. Most of the mainstream media refused to cover the investigation, but journalists from the Detroit Free Press conducted their own examination of the material and found no evidence of deceit or untruthful statements. This was the closest look yet at the destructive level of atrocities against the Vietnamese people.

At the end, the cost to life in the Vietnam War was higher than all of America's previous wars combined. As many as two million South and North Vietnamese civilians were killed and the number of American soldiers dead was estimated at thirty-one thousand. More than two hundred thousand were wounded. On all sides, a number greater than three million died.

* * *

RU members were expected to practice target shooting at least once monthly, but in fact, that happened sporadically and always when I was on campus or otherwise occupied. In truth, I was ducking the responsibility. Firing a gun in any scenario just didn't seem like something I could do. My absence escaped notice until the day Lance, our trainer, caught up with me. He made me commit to being outside my house the next morning at eight a.m., ready to go. When he arrived, I was still in bed. Joe was gone, likely to an early meeting. Buffy yawned widely and stuck her head under the blankets.

"Hey, comrade lazy bones!" His voice was convivial, amused.

I wiped my eyes, crusty as always first thing in the morning. "Shit, Lance, I slept through my alarm. Give me a minute."

I jumped up and fell back just as quickly. "Whoa, too fast."

"You okay?" he asked.

I never had headaches but that morning my head was pounding. I attributed it to staying up into the early hours printing a leaflet that announced yet another lunchtime rally against the war.

"Yeah. Throw me those clothes over there." I pointed to the shirt and jeans left on a chair.

It was a hazy morning with few clouds, the sun glaring hot. Two guys from the workers collective sat in the back seat; I got into the front. Lance drove us to a long-abandoned field, dry and corrugated from the fierce winds off the coast, only a few miles from the San Jose airport. Overhead, a flock of crows screeched while airplanes circled in a queue for landing. Other than some crumbling outbuildings, piles of rusted farm implements scattered helter-skelter, and clusters of weedy wildflowers, the field was empty.

I felt the heat but chills dug into my spine. My eyeballs ached in the bright light.

"Hey, Jody, you don't look too good." Lance touched the back of his hand to my cheek. "Jesus, you're burning up."

"I'm okay, Lance."

He shook his head. "I'll take you home. You should just sleep it off." I knew he was right, but hated to give in to what I considered weakness.

Once back in my bedroom, the clothes I wore dropped back to the chair. By the time I crawled between the sheets, settling into my body's impression still there from less than an hour before, it hurt to swallow. Chills turned to sweat and back again.

I was sure it was my fault. Getting sick to get out of shooting a gun sounded like something I would do. But as the day went on and I couldn't stop shaking, I no longer doubted I was truly ill. When Joe returned home, he went out again to buy chicken broth and bread to make toast. He still cared for me in his way, and that day I was grateful for his sympathy.

Several weeks later, Lance and I made plans again, this time for just the two of us. Once at the field, we rearranged the two haystacks already out there and fronted them with paper body outlines, a red circle around the heart. Crows cawed above us as though they'd never left.

He first brought out a 12-gauge shotgun. "It has a wide spray so a bit easier to hit your mark even if your aim is off."

Lance held it out for me to take, but my hands remained at my side.

"What is it, Jody? You really don't want to be here, do you?" He lit a cigarette and leaned back against the car.

I took his matches and lit one of my own. My hands were shaking. I might have lied if it had been anyone else, but it wasn't hard to be honest with Lance.

"Guns freak me out, they scare me. I'm a pacifist, or at least once was. But the only reason to learn how to shoot one is if you have to use it, right? Then what? Their aim is better, their hands are steadier, they see me before I see them? Or, I see them but I can't find it in myself to fire? It's just so alien to me." This was before the anticipated shoot-out at my house.

"My dad gave me a .22 when I was eight. We hunted together. But regardless of our past, you and me, we've made a commitment to be military-ready for the revolution. You have to decide which side you're on. You can't pick and choose the part you'll play."

I knew I had already made that choice—there was nothing more to say. I ground out the cigarette under my heel and hefted the shotgun, feeling its weight and stroking the smooth barrel. Forcing a smile, I said, "I'll have you know I was a sharpshooter, top of the charts, at the arcade when I was twelve. Five ducks in a row!"

"Wow, five? Impressive. Picture ducks on those outlines and you'll do fine!"

We donned eye protection over our glasses. Lance showed me how to balance the gun on my arm, tuck the butt in my shoulder, and how the pump mechanism worked. He warned me about the harsh recoil and that the scope might jump up, one reason for the eyewear. We donned earmuffs.

The early morning heat bubbled from the ground in mirage-like swirls, dripping sweat into my eyes, making it difficult to sight the target. When I finally pulled the trigger, my eyes closed reflexively. Pellets sprayed far from the target. The kickback, so much harsher than I expected, knocked my shoulder hard and numbed my hand. Lance encouraged me to try again. This time he stood behind me, helping to steady the gun, and I shot a second time. Even with the muffs on, the shot boomed like a lighthouse horn next to my ears. Soaked with sweat, I knew I had to do it again, this time on my own, and around the fifth try, I laughed when I hit the target somewhere over the spleen.

Lance also had rifles and he patiently explained their advantages. The kickback wasn't so much and they were lighter weight. I tried the 30-ought-6, the rifle preferred by snipers, like the one Joe hid under our bed. It had a long barrel and was easier to handle than the shotgun, but still, my aim was lousy. The third, an M1 like the other rifle under our bed, was favored by the American Armed Services. I had better luck with the shorter barrel; at least four bullets hit the target's legs or arms. I kept at it, getting used to keeping both eyes open. Much later, my arms and legs fatigued, Lance congratulated me, knowing how hard I'd worked at keeping my aversion under control.

His praise overjoyed me. I felt triumphant and couldn't deny that I found firing the guns exciting. Still, I couldn't mentally make the leap from hitting targets to shooting at cops. That challenge was yet to come.

Joe and I didn't officially break up but he was drafted into the army, and the RU decided it a good opportunity for him to organize within the armed forces. A party was held for him the night before he left for basic training in Fort Lewis, Washington. Although our relationship had withered to nothing, I still longed for one last connection and asked him to join me in the bathroom for a private conversation. We sat together on the side of the bathtub. I don't recall what was said, only that a simple goodbye kiss deepened. I remember wanting him and it seemed he wanted me too, but somebody knocked on the door and the moment passed.

14

FEAR

Late in January, 1970, a Central Committee meeting was to be held at a camp owned by the University of California in Cazadero near the Russian River. An ideological split within the Revolutionary Union was threatening, and a vote would be taken whether or not to expel the rebellious faction. As an underling, I would likely not be a participant but numbers were needed to support the San Jose status quo and so a few of us lower in the ranks were asked to come.

Barry Greenberg, for reasons I couldn't fathom, chose me to drive him there in my roommate's Volkswagen. I didn't want to be alone with him—a stern man similar in personality to my father, he made me nervous and difficult to be myself. I tried to get others to take my place but nobody stepped up. Along the way he was tense, writing notes as I drove, only speaking to give directions and ask me not to smoke and turn the radio off. I didn't know what to do with myself—my nature wasn't made for this silent submissive task. We stopped for gas on the mountain road outside Guerneville. Once we headed out, the curves we'd been crawling along straightened out and I shifted from second into third, then into fourth. Or so I thought. Loud clanging, louder grinding metal on metal. The car jolted to a stop.

I looked at Barry. His face purpled. I thought he might strike me.

"Shit, you threw a rod! You were in second!"

"No, I wasn't," I snapped back. I knew immediately that he was right, but I couldn't admit it. This need to lie in self-defense sprang from deep within me. I'd learned well from living with my mother—always deny. In many ways it had served me well.

He got out of the car and I waited, afraid to move, while he walked back to the gas station where he somehow arranged a car to rent. Within an hour we were on our way, this time Barry behind the wheel. The silence was thick—if only I could have disappeared. Once we arrived at the site, I hurried away from him as fast as I could but told nobody what happened. I was too appalled, too angry with myself, and most of all, too embarrassed.

While the higher-ups battled out ideology and semantics, I sat with my other low-level comrades trying to follow the arguments. The controversy was between one faction led by Bruce Franklin, a professor at Stanford and one of the RU founders, who believed that the proletariat's political consciousness was sufficiently high to begin waging the guerilla warfare phase of revolution. The national faction, led by Bob Avakian along with the San Jose bloc led by Barry, said no, that we should be increasing our efforts to educate the working class because the tools of production and the systems of communication were still in the hands of the bosses. They deemed it necessary to continue building the revolutionary movement through study and recruitment. The rebels were based in Palo Alto—I'd never met any of them.

At the end of the weekend a vote was called—to turn the RU

over to the more radical agenda or to expel those ready to pick up guns. My cadre was called in to add to the votes to stay the course. The Palo Alto faction split away, now calling themselves *Venceremos* (not connected to the revolutionary international brigade in Cuba). The organizational tumult that followed didn't trouble me—I far preferred the ideal of further education vs. guerilla actions.

This vote turned out to be a historic split in the revolutionary movement, much noted in articles and books written about the times. Four years later, the San Jose Revolutionary Union would join Bob Avakian in Chicago, renaming themselves the Revolutionary Communist Party.

Regardless of the upheaval, I remained as committed as ever. In early March, our student collective was meeting in a second-story apartment near the college east of downtown San Jose. It belonged to two boys, Terry and Mike, also from Southern California. Taped on the walls were the requisite posters of college revolutionaries—Vladimir Lenin, Malcolm X, Mao, and Bobby Seale. Scattered political pamphlets, record albums, and a dry philodendron drooping yellow leaves sat atop unpainted boards stacked on cinder blocks.

The meeting's agenda intended to discuss fundraising for comrades who were jailed the day before following another demonstration against the war. Someone knocked at the door and I jumped up to open it, but Charles restrained me.

"Who is it?" he yelled.

"It's Charles. Open up!" We looked at each other, shaking our heads. Not our Charles, who was in the apartment, right next to me.

Charles asked, "Charles who?"

"Open up!" There was more hammering. "Police!"

"Let's see a warrant. Slide it under the door," somebody demanded.

In response, the door was kicked open. Policemen dressed in riot gear surged in, guns drawn, herding us with nightsticks outside to the landing. This was just the action we expected that night when we sat armed in my living room more than two years before.

"Face the wall, arms overhead!"

We lined up side by side, fingers spread wide against the white glitter stucco. My eyes locked on the smoke curling from the cigarette I let drop. There were eight or nine of us, more than fifteen of them. Two men in suits stood back in observation. We later found out that they were from the District Attorney's office.

"You! Hands down, behind your back! Now!" yelled a voice behind me. I thought the command was directed to Terry, just to my right. I turned to him, my face drawing into an expression of concern, but it was me they wanted. My hands were grabbed and pulled down and back, my wrists handcuffed so quickly that my thoughts tumbled, unable to keep up with what was happening.

They also cuffed David and Gerry. David resisted, mocking the police, but they overcame him. So brave, I thought, reminding me that we were righteous and the cops were pigs. The boys preened and strutted as though chosen for a prize, while I tried not to let tears betray my fear. A beefy hand clamped on my shoulder to steer me down the single flight of stairs. Students brought out by the revolving red and blue lights crowded the sidewalk.

A girl recognized me and shouted out my name. A chant erupted: "Free Jody, Free Jody!" That buoyed me until the cop toppled me into the back seat of his cruiser and slammed the door shut. The front seat was pushed so far back that it was impossible to right myself without my hands and so I stayed bent as though planted in loose dirt.

I was the only girl arrested that night. The boys were brought to another car. Alone, bound and caged in the back of a pig car, I was very afraid, hyperaware that my life at that moment was in the hands of my sworn enemies.

The two older cops in the front seat left the curb with tires screeching, siren screaming, lights revolving blue and red. I was wearing bellbottoms and a Mexican peasant blouse whose wide short sleeves revealed I neither shaved nor wore a bra, not looking at all like the majority of girls who in those days still wore sweater sets. By the way they squinted their eyes at me in the rearview mirror, their bloodless lips pressed tight with contempt, I had no doubt that they despised me.

Monotone squawks sizzled from the radio, a female voice breaking up, something about needing cars—somewhere a burglary was occurring. Too quickly, the car was away from city lights, passing fields where only days before the RU joined migrant workers organizing for the U.F.W. Just twelve minutes from downtown, the area would soon be a development complete with mall and freeway, but then it was grassland and sagebrush drowned at night in pervasive darkness.

The cop at the wheel asked his partner, "What do you think? This a good place?"

"Yeah. Do it."

"Do what?" I asked.

The top and head lights were turned off as the car spun to the right onto hard dirt pitted with rocks and chuckholes. The driver didn't decrease his speed, just kept bouncing deeper and deeper into the gloom.

He said, "They'll never find her."

"Not that anyone would care," his partner said, laughing.

Their disembodied voices were casual, making what was happening all the more frightening. Never had I felt so vulnerable, not even when my father was raging.

Trapped in the narrow space, I was painfully aware that the all-powerful pigs could do whatever they wanted to me. Picturing the worst—violent rape, buried alive—images of my funeral, my mother stoic, my father ashen, my comrades holding high a red flag, surged with my panic.

After what seemed like hours, though couldn't have been more than ten minutes, lights appeared ahead. The car suddenly slowed and swerved onto asphalt, turning in a wide arc in front of a hangar-sized brick building. Milpitas-Elmwood Women's Correctional Facility. My breath released in hiccupping gasps. The driver stopped short, slamming my face into the back of his seat, bloodying my nose. They laughed—it was all a joke to them. Still, I was so grateful to get there safely that I had to bite my tongue not to thank them.

Pulled from the car and pushed through the front door, my blood dripped a trail from the entry to the booking desk. The handcuffs were removed—the charges against me read. Malicious mischief and disturbing the peace while leading an anti-ROTC demonstration on campus the week before. I wondered at the time why they hadn't busted me. I certainly gave them cause after I stood on a platform in the campus quad, holding a microphone to urge the crowd to circle the bungalow where representatives from the U.S. Army, Navy, and Marines were interviewing prospective members. We beat on the Quonset hut they were housed in, pitting the corrugated walls with our fists and rocks, all the while chanting: *ROTC must go!*

In the school newspaper, an article reporting the protest said: "Jody Forrester, SJLF (San Jose Liberation Front) member, said triumphantly, "We disrupted them. That's what we were trying to do."

The matron at the front desk handed me a wet paper towel to clean my face, then took my picture. This time I knew the drill. She pressed my inked fingers within five squares on a form she held flat.

"Wait on the bench over there." She pointed at the wall in front of her. "You'll be assigned a bed in a while."

My shaking slowly ebbed and panic transmuted to anger. I wished again I were more like David who, I'm sure, was telling the pigs what would happen to them once WE were in charge. Instead I stewed, vacillating between frustration and fear—the pigs still had the upper hand, but the presence of the desk matron with her maternal soft smile and bright blue eyes reassured me. I wanted to tell her how badly the cops had scared me but resisted, reminding myself that she may be nice but was still a pig.

A girl wearing a navy blue jumpsuit was brought out and told to sit next to me while she waited for a phone call to come through.

"What'd they pick you up for?" she asked. She didn't seem to notice the blood staining my shirt.

"Disturbing the peace at a demonstration at San Jose State against ROTC recruiters."

She looked at me more closely, her confusion clear.

"You know, anti-war?"

Her eyes shifted, pencil-thin brows lifting. She was probably my age and pretty in a way I'd always envied—long blond surfer hair, wide-set blue eyes, and skin that likely never knew a blemish.

"For real?" she asked. I saw that to her I might have spoken in Latin. Before I could explain, the payphone rang.

She talked quickly and I could only make out that she was telling somebody to come get her out. Once she hung up, the matron escorted her through a reinforced steel door. I never saw her again.

I was still on the bench, feeling like I did when waiting outside the high school principal's office, rehearsing what I'd say when given the chance. A well-dressed man came through the door, and from the desk the matron pointed him toward me. He told me he was sent by Barry Greenberg to post my bail. Noting the blood, he asked if the police struck me, then took a picture with his Polaroid even though I told him they hadn't.

I went to the bathroom to wash my face and hands before walking out with him. His car was a new Cadillac, the same model my father aspired to own. I paused—the car represented the middle-class trappings that I loathed, but I was grateful to be liberated so said nothing.

15

BETRAYED

Joe was still at basic training when the lease came up at our house. In the spring of 1971, I was pulled aside by RU leadership and directed to move into a two-bedroom apartment with a couple that were members of the workers' collective. It was thought that it would be a good idea for me to live with people who were actualizing their commitment to the proletariat. Brian worked at a fiberglass manufacturing plant; Jane was at the phone company. Their apartment was far more put together than I was used to—matching dishes, serving platters, a full set of cutlery. Red geraniums and yellow marigolds fronted the grey squat building. Although my student comrades might have cringed, I liked the quiet domesticity.

The problem was Buffy. She had a backyard at our previous house, but here in the apartment she ripped up the carpet at the front door with her incessant scrabbling to get out when I was away. My new roommates hated her. After four months, they asked me to leave. I moved near the college to a two-bedroom to live with my closest friends in the student collective. Pamela and

I slept on a steel military bunk bed in one room, Meg on a twin bed in the other.

My parents were no longer willing to help me financially after I told them I'd left college. They were very upset, and although it was a lie, I assured them I was only taking a leave of absence. Although they still knew nothing about my being in the Revolutionary Union, they knew by then how committed I was to ending the Vietnam War, and understood that to me it was a priority, at least for the spring semester.

I began piecing together a living with a series of short-lived jobs. I haven't any memory of how I ended up hawking in a booth at the Santa Clara County Fair for one blistering hot Labor Day weekend. The carnival world was unlike anything I had known before or since, both fascinating and repulsive. The permanent workers, owners of the rides and booths, lived in a subculture as different from me as could be.

The fair manager assigned me to a game with glass plates assembled in four rows of six. The man who owned it, an old-time carny named Brett, made no effort to get to know me or to let me know him. I got it. While he slept year-round in a trailer, carting his booth county to county, I was just passing through.

Fairgoers tossed dimes and those that stuck on a plate won a stuffed animal, but most slid off. Once he was sure I knew what I was doing, Brett left me on my own.

"One thin dime! That's all it takes to win here! Just one dime! We've got pink bears! We've got purple hippos! We've got blue tigers! C'mon! One thin dime!" Until my voice wore out, I shouted to every passerby.

On the second day, I arrived an hour early to have some time to look around, but first went to my assigned booth. I saw Brett running a cloth over the surface of a plate, cleaning it, I thought, but then I saw a can of Crisco. I suppose I shouldn't have been surprised he greased the plates, but I was.

"Brett, what the hell?"

He glanced over, not seeming to recognize me at first, but then he did.

"Get outta here! You're fired!" The look he gave me threatened enough that I turned away, fuming that I had no recourse. Who could I tell?

My next job was at a motel that rented rooms by the hour, although I didn't understand what that meant during the interview, not until my first day. Scrubbing sinks, tubs, and toilets. Changing linen. It was both novel and disgusting. The sheets were often stained with blood, cum, and wine. I stayed with it for several weeks, until I could no longer stand to clean the same room three times a day.

Thanks to my mother, who insisted I take two years of typing and bookkeeping in high school as a "fallback just in case," my other jobs, obtained through a temporary agency, were usually as a typist or file clerk. Food stamps supplemented my income, as they did my roommates and other comrades in the student collective.

* * *

I knew that we were supposed to repress our personal needs for political gain, but the rules went out the window when, through mutual friends, I met Alex from Berkeley. His classically Italian face was a type I'd always gravitated toward—strong cheekbones, dark olive skin, thick black wavy hair.

Alex's practiced seduction made me feel confident and attractive in a way I hadn't yet experienced with a man. Still stung in the wake of Joe's rejection, I was easily persuaded to sleep with him. Only nineteen, and still relatively naïve about men, I took him back to my apartment.

Pamela was away so we had my room to ourselves. In the narrow top bunk, Alex made love expertly and once again I fell into a fantasy about a future with a man I barely knew except that he fit the dream.

The next morning, while still in bed, Alex sat up, looked at me and laughed. Caught in the afterglow of a night of lovemaking, I laughed too.

Then he spoke. "I can't wait 'til I'm back in Berkeley. Man, nobody will believe I balled a member of the Revolutionary Union!" He told me with a smile too wide that he was a member of our rival political group, the Progressive Labor Party, and it was the RU he wanted to fuck, not me. His cruelty crushed me, but I blamed myself more than him. Once again I lost my head, heart, and body to a pretty boy.

I didn't want anybody to know, but when I missed my period, I had to tell my collective. They roundly chastised me for breaking protocol, but agreed with me that an abortion was the only solution. The pregnancy felt more like a tumor that had to be excised than a potential child. I only wanted it to go away. Confused and scared, I didn't tell Alex—I didn't even know how to reach him—but what good would it do? Chances were he'd crow about his virility.

This was in 1971, when Roe vs. Wade was wending its way to the Supreme Court. Hospital abortions in California were permitted to women who could prove to two psychiatrists that their mental health was at risk. Based on the doctors' recommendations, a medical committee that met bimonthly would decide their fate.

I scheduled an appointment to see the first psychiatrist available at Kaiser Permanente, the hospital where my parents maintained my health insurance. I remember the doctor in bits: large-framed thick glasses, an immaculate white coat, shirt collar drooping off a wattled neck. On his desk a stained white coffee cup sat next to a photograph of five kids, all brown-skinned like their East Indian father. A framed diploma from Harvard Medical School hung on the wall behind him displaying the insignia of *summa cum laude*. I sat on the chair opposite him wearing an ill-fitting Salvation Army pleated skirt and white polyester ruffled blouse purchased just that morning.

He asked questions about my health history, age, date of first period, and then the obvious. "Why do you want an abortion?"

Long practiced at arranging my personality and speech depending on my audience, I told him I wasn't yet ready to have a baby, that I had aspirations to be a doctor myself. I lied easily, going on to tell him my goal was to attend my father's alma mater, Stanford Medical School (my father was an insurance broker), then join his internal medicine practice once I was licensed. The rest of our session was spent discussing Harvard vs. Stanford.

Before we parted, the doctor shook my hand and told me what a pleasure it was to meet such an ambitious, articulate young woman. I wouldn't have to make an appointment with the second psychiatrist, he said, he'll take care of everything. Sure enough, the procedure was given approval just before my tenth week.

On the day scheduled, the sun pigmented the oft-polluted San Jose skies a deep cerulean blue. Everyone in my student neighborhood was wearing shorts and sandals, except me—again wearing Salvation Army clothes, this time polyester forest green pants with an elastic waist and a T-shirt with surfers on the front. Pamela drove me to the hospital, leaving me outside the double glass doors of the monolithic concrete six-storied structure. I checked in with admissions and was weighed on a scale in the hall. A nurse midwife shaved my pubic hair in a bathroom. I didn't like being handled like that, but I did as I was told, reminding myself over and over again that I was there by choice.

The narrow bed that I waited on was in a room with three others, all young girls like me. A weeping mother stood by the side of one, a worried boyfriend by another. The girl in the next bed over was alone. I wanted to say something to her, just to normalize the abnormality of why we were there, but I didn't—nothing about that day was normal. It struck me, as it always did when confined, that outside the un-curtained windows were people walking and driving by with no idea what was happening inside. The isolation unnerved me. I was too much on my own, without allies, nobody near that cared.

A nurse came to my bedside with a triplicate form on a clipboard.

"It's a list of possible side effects of the procedure, but nothing usually happens, nothing to worry about. Just sign at the bottom where it states you understand the risks."

Blood clots, heavy or prolonged bleeding, damage to cervix, death.

"Death? You're kidding, right?"

"It rarely happens," she said.

She knew I would sign. Again, the choice was taken out of my hands and in truth I was grateful to be in a hospital. It was only a couple of years before when my closest friend in high school had an illegal abortion. The procedure was done on a living room table and left her hemorrhaging. Two days later, her brother took her to a hospital where she recovered after two pints of blood infusions.

One and then another bed was rolled out. I crossed my fingers, wishing I had a beloved entity to pray to.

My turn. The surgery room was brightly lit—no shadows, all business. My legs were lifted and placed on icy metal supports. A nurse squeezed my hand. "It'll be over before you know it." I squeezed back, anchoring myself to the comfort of her warmth. The anesthesiologist put a cone over my mouth and nose, instructing me to count backward. The next thing I knew, I was throwing up and shaking madly in a different bed, in a different room.

"It's normal," the comforting nurse said, "a response to the general anesthetic."

"Am I still pregnant?" I asked while the nurse took my blood pressure. She shook her head. Unwanted tears threatened.

"It's over, dear. Too late for regrets."

She misunderstood me. It was the half-hour gone by that gnawed at me. I needed details to fill in the blanks. Where was the baby, how did they extract it? What I couldn't stand was that I was knocked out while others were indifferent witnesses to such a huge event in my life. No answers were forthcoming. The nurse was already off to the next bed.

I stayed overnight in the hospital, visited by nobody, and cried often, self-pity amplifying my loneliness. I wanted my mother, not the mother I had, but the made-up mother I often turned to when I needed consoling.

Late the next morning, I waited by the exit in a wheelchair the nurses demanded I stay in until Pamela brought her car around. Although it was recommended I rest for another day or two, I insisted she take me to a noontime collective meeting already scheduled. I wanted to prove to my comrades that despite my bad judgment in sleeping with Alex, nothing would get in the way of my revolutionary zeal. I needed them to witness my courage, resiliency, and strength, and be impressed that I didn't permit myself even a moment of sadness or self-pity to interfere with our agenda.

Once there, I waved away solicitous greetings, then felt abandoned and rejected as they moved on to the next item. Just like that, the last twenty-four hours, like the pregnancy itself, were obliterated.

16

AWARENESS

Women's Liberation hatched organically from the Civil Rights and anti-Vietnam War movements. By 1971, though still centered in the population of white educated women, the struggle was gaining momentum. Consciousness-raising meetings became the norm during which personal issues were politicized. The focus was on educating society to the oppression of women in daily life, while emphasis was put on women having the freedom to make choices in defiance of the long-held standard of patriarchy and ingrained sexism.

Within the RU, I wanted to have something to do that was uniquely mine so I suggested to my collective that they assign me to an off-campus women's group. I was convinced that the new wave of feminism was a ripe base to recruit from. They hesitated, reminding me that Mao's ideology clearly stated that the liberation of woman could only be achieved by joining with all citizens to defeat capitalism and imperialism.

"What is pretty much missing in Women's Liberation is a class analysis of the nature of women's oppression, which would be my role as a communist to bring into the meetings' discussions. Our struggles as women can only go so far without taking on political dimensions."

Convinced, Charles said, "Okay, Jody. Give it a try. We'll want weekly updates."

Once at the SJS women's group, with about a dozen women attending, I found pretty quickly that they were too busy discovering what it meant to be female in a man's world to care about a proletarian uprising, In fact, they questioned my membership in a male-dominated organization. My intention to convince them that the status of women was intricately tied to the struggle against capitalist control diminished as I began to realize that I had never thought of myself as female, as one of many, or thought of my need for men's approval as anything but my personal failing. Yes, women earning less than men incensed me, opportunities denied outraged me, but I'd thought of women's liberation as political and irrelevant to me personally.

Soon they brought me into their discussions and self-searching rather than my leading with a class analysis. When it did occur to me, I decided that would come later. Something was happening that I both wanted and needed to explore.

We met in a house close to campus belonging to a Ph.D. candidate in education. Her small living room was edged with books, both piled on the floor and on boards supported by red bricks. The group sat in a circle on the orange shag carpet ubiquitous in rental homes and apartments. It was an intimate gathering, no real agenda, no real order, mostly the outpouring of women feeling safe with each other. We talked about men's domination in our lives and our vulnerability to self-subjugation.

It was as if my brain switched on, and without forethought, I was all the way in with my own stories. The babysitter when I was six who stuck his penis in my mouth. My after-school job at sixteen when my boss ran his fingers up my leg under the miniskirt I wore. The times my breasts were grabbed by men walking past me on the sidewalk. Despite the differences in our economic level, age, and body type, everybody had at least one story of similar aggression.

A Woman's Liberation group was not supposed to be the place where I learned for the first time that women could not only have orgasms but could arouse themselves to orgasm. How all my life I had missed that vital information, I had no idea. A feminist magazine named *RAT* had a full-page drawing of women's genitals and a detailed description on how to masturbate. At night, in my top bunk, I followed the instructions one by one as though piecing together a balsa airplane.

Eventually I reported success and the others cheered. Yay me!

Much of our conversations centered on personal freedom, especially in regard to our bodies. As in W.L.F. meetings nationwide, we examined our cervixes with plastic speculums and a mirror, and talked about pleasuring ourselves rather than relying on men. Where in that conversation could I bring up the topic of armed struggle and working-class rule? It seemed impossible and I increasingly felt conflicted, although it was also impossible to explain to my collective why I failed.

"What could be the problem?" my comrades, both men and women, asked. "Talk to them about China. It was the revolution that freed women to be equal to men."

"But this isn't China and these women are struggling with personal complexities and abusive relationships within their families and with men at their workplace. How do I connect the personal with the political?"

This dilemma wasn't new—it was already brewing at the core of the struggle I had with our ideology, even after the additional study my collective recommended I read.

I hoped for advice, but nobody got my confusion. I invited one of the more mature female comrades from the community collective to come to a meeting, hoping she could help me figure this out, but she kept cancelling—I was on my own.

After that, when an update was asked for, I kept it simple. "I'm making inroads. The women are starting to trust me. It'll take time."

I doubted my collective would congratulate me for learning how to make myself come.

17

DISILLUSIONED

The women's group disbanded after less than a year when several of the participants graduated or were too busy with other commitments. Although I continued to find meaning in my time with them, I was still primarily engaged in the active protests led by the RU.

Vietnam continued to be a major source of offshore oil fields that Standard Oil exploited. The Revolutionary Union held a rally on campus urging people to protest at the oil company's local offices against their complicity with American imperialism. Although we leafleted the campus and community, calling on anti-war protesters to rally with us, only twenty showed, mostly RU members. Undeterred, we walked in a large circle near the entrance, brandishing posters and chanting: *Big oil out of Vietnam!*

Standard Oil's satellite research facility was housed in a two-story brick building fronted by dozens of windows. Gunmetal grey river rocks lined the perimeter of the crew-cut front lawn, white and purple impatiens growing among them. David, as usual, threw the first rock through a second-story window.

Others followed. The noise of breaking glass excited me and for the first time I wanted to join in, but when I threw a rock it didn't fly more than ten feet before tumbling to the ground. Embarrassed by my weak arm, I moved to the sidewalk, lit a cigarette, and looked up.

Instead of seeing what I expected, men in suits at the windows, there were only women in dresses gaping down at us. They looked like my mother and aunts, all of whom worked as secretaries at one time in their lives. My comrades were too close to the building to see inside the windows—they thought the rocks were trashing Standard Oil, not women working at their typewriters. I was the only spectator and mortified at our betrayal of the very workers we were meant to be championing. I yelled to my comrades but they couldn't hear me over the bedlam so I ran closer, but before I could alert them, sirens approached and we scattered.

I was upset and told the two people in my car what I'd observed. They were sober in their agreement that our actions were unconscionable and urged me to bring it up at the start of our meeting later that night.

I was ready until I walked into Charles's apartment and saw Barry Greenberg sitting in the living room in an overstuffed armchair looking none too pleased. He rarely came to one of our meetings and I was sure the others were as uneasy as I was.

He called on me right away to explain what had occurred that afternoon.

I didn't expect to be singled out. Everyone turned to me; they had no idea what was going on. He nodded for me to begin. I had intended to talk to my collective only—how did Barry find out? But then I realized, of course, one of the people in the car must have told him. I was in the tenth grade again, asked by the principal to tell him who else was with me when I stole cigarettes from a store nearby.

I took a breath. "First let me apologize to my collective. I had planned on talking this through with you tonight and would not on my own have chosen to involve leadership." I had to get that out of the way. "But, okay. Out at Standard Oil today, we were throwing rocks through windows where the typing pool was working." I warmed up, the words queuing in an orderly line on my tongue.

"Are they not workers, albeit not blue-collar? Should they have to bear the brunt of their employer's evil?" I liked the sound of that last line, thought it smart and well said and was mostly relieved that I could speak two sentences without tripping over my words.

Barry was rightfully furious at our lack of reconnaissance, at our presumptuous attack of those too far down the economic chain to influence policy. Heads hung. He was the stern father, we his disruptive children failing to live up to his expectations. He spelled out how our short-termed actions were not helpful in lieu of revolutionary planning, and demanded that David come before the regional committee to review his role in leadership. Barry reminded us that Lenin said:

> *Lacking an analytical approach, many of our comrades do not want to go deeply into complex matters, to analyze and study them over and over again, but like to draw simple conclusions that are either absolutely affirmative or absolutely negative. From now on we should remedy this state of affairs.*

Before leaving, he assigned reading of that chapter of Lenin's collected works to be discussed at our next meeting. Deflated after he left, we abandoned our agenda. Nobody objected when

Terry lit a joint or when David brought out a six-pack of Budweiser. Craig and Ken sat at the kitchen table arguing ideology; I lounged on the sofa, watching spirals of pot and cigarette smoke bouncing off the ceiling like bubbles blown from a wand.

I remember singing along to John Lennon's "All You Need is Love," and telling Terry about the time when I had no doubt loving one another was the solution to the world's misery. He understood; he was also from Los Angeles.

It was driven home to me how much I had changed. Armed revolution, not love, was the answer and I couldn't understand why even my longtime friends in Los Angeles weren't willing to embrace communism for a society of women and men of all colors and cultures influencing policy. Why couldn't they see how much better we would be once capitalism was defeated? They argued that I was on a narrow ideological shelf, that sleeping with guns under my bed with the intent to use them in violent revolution would make no difference to a country run by greedy profiteers. I wavered in the face of their objections, which revealed further how ambivalent I felt about using guns to foment revolution.

After two years as a member, I still battled internally with aspects of our Maoist ideology. While much made sense to me intellectually, I continued to be unable to speak comfortably with people thought to be potential recruits. The worst of this occurred when I was in Maria Dolores's house. I wanted to, I really did, but when push came to shove I clammed up, too self-conscious to interject theory into casual conversations. It seemed near impossible for me to embody the necessary detachment and emotional distance required of a genuine communist. It wasn't enough to know I was right; I needed confidence to convince others.

The collective knew that I was struggling and suggested I

participate in a criticism/self-criticism review. Mao Tse-Tung deemed these sessions most important, a time for critical accounting that would afford us the opportunity to better ourselves, to assess where improvement was needed, and define what was working and what was not.

The collective secretary recorded the following:

Comrade Jody is greeted and asked to read what she's written.

I was nervous, all attention on me. I lit a cigarette, coughed, put it out.

The principal contradiction in my work is the desire to be a good communist versus selfishness and self-centeredness. I continue to value friendships over the mass line and allow my self-consciousness to silence my voice as a representative of the RU.

Also, a serious contradiction develops around the question of leadership. I feel inadequate to the tasks set by the collective and feel too much pressure by my comrades to maintain a leadership image.

CM (Charles): What would you say are your strengths as a revolutionary?

JF: I am devoted and have confidence and faith in the organization and its purpose. I listen to what people have to say and make an effort to contextualize their concerns as part of the larger class struggle.

CM: And your weaknesses?

JF: A tendency toward individualism, to allow personal relationships to divert me from my work among the masses. I don't really know how to put into practice our beliefs in Marxist-Leninist-Mao Tse-Tung thought. I have faith in the masses in theory, but also feel fear when among the masses, becoming more concerned about sounding stupid than about communicating.

The meeting's response:

The collective agrees with Comrade Jody's analysis of herself and her principal contradiction. We propose that in order to combat lack of self-confidence she should take part in an intensive study group as theory is her major weakness and, at the same time, combat her bourgeois self-interest through ideological struggle in our meetings.

Comrade Jody is valued for her leadership and diligence, both in mass work and as a speaker. She is to be commended for assigning herself the task of joining a SJS women's consciousness-raising group with the intention of bringing mass line to the group.

More discussion followed and, with huge relief, I found that there were more people beside me struggling with the same questions. Only now do I recall that we were all women. It was a truism on the Left that men and women were no different, but in reality, the expectation held that women should act like men— linear in our thinking, suppressing emotional responses, practicing exclusivity rather than inclusivity. When I chided myself for not being a better communist, I see now I was chiding myself for not being a better man.

18

ABANDONED

Although the self-criticism session did much to revive me, in the long run nothing changed. I was beginning to question more deeply whether I could continue to represent the party line. If not, I thought, maybe I had no business putting myself forward as a communist. Being locked into this singular mindset isolated me from my peers in a way I couldn't help thinking about when I looked around and observed the rites of passage that others my age were experiencing. I wondered who I might be if I allowed myself to pave my own way, to think for myself. It's not that I no longer saw Maoism as a viable way to bring much-needed change to the United States; it was more that I was beginning to feel I might no longer be capable of being a revolutionary to the exclusion of everything else.

In February 1972, soon after my twentieth birthday, my collective was invited to attend a party in San Francisco given by the American Communist Party to celebrate Angela Davis's recent release from sixteen months in prison. Davis was a leading African-American activist, a Communist Party member, and close to the Black Panthers. That morning, Melissa, an old and dear friend from Los Angeles, came up to San Jose to visit me. It was only after she arrived that my roommates reminded me I should have gotten permission from the collective for her visit. Surprised that I had been so sloppy, I was also embarrassed in front of Melissa, who knew me when I made my own decisions.

Feeling rebellious, I brought her to San Francisco with me without informing the collective chairman, rationalizing that the party was a public event. Looking back, I see that the fissure was already widening in my commitment to the Revolutionary Union, that in my defiance, I was essentially saying "fuck you."

The storefront in the Mission District brimmed with celebrants waiting for Davis to arrive. Collective members, as always, were meant to talk up the Revolutionary Union's party line, especially in contrast with the Communist Party, but the music was loud and people were dancing. Melissa and I stood near the edge, me drinking water, her drinking a beer. The band had me swaying and tapping my foot until I grabbed her, pulling her onto the dance floor.

She was a high school friend with whom I had taken a lot of acid and we fell pretty quickly into steps from those psychedelic days, mirroring each other as we swirled with arms overhead, making witchy eyes. Our friendship had been strained by the radical turn my life had taken and it felt wonderful to reconnect.

The room was muggy hot. A few boisterous songs later, I went outside and found a place to sit on a graffiti-smeared block wall to light a cigarette. The street was quiet and peaceful, a welcome respite from the crowd inside. Just as I snuffed out my smoke, three Chicano boys, high school-age, came outside and asked me for a light.

I was digging in my pocket for matches when one of the boys pushed me to the ground. Light cast from the street lamp reflected off his boot's steel toes. The first kick landed and a crunch sounded in my chest. More followed, amplified by shouts that they were going to kill me.

"Fucking faggot, fudge packer, queer," they yelled.

It didn't sink in right away that they thought I was a gay man, but as soon as it did, I tried to let them know, screaming, "I'm a girl. Stop, please!"

I scuttled away from one just to be kicked by another. One boy, he didn't look much older than thirteen, stamped his heel in my crotch over and over again. I folded my head and knees into my chest, pleading with them, trying to make them hear.

"Please, stop, I'm a girl, I'm a girl." But their steel-toed kicks didn't let up. Maybe thirty seconds passed, for sure less than sixty, before Melissa came out and ran them off when she screamed.

I wanted to stay on the ground, but she pulled me up and inside. Clutching my chest, bent over, I expelled deep gulps of breath to stifle my moans.

"Call the police!" Melissa shouted. "Some guys jumped her!"

It was the quiet moment between songs. Everybody looked over and a few came close, wanting to know what happened, but they were quickly pushed away by an upper echelon RU member who rushed over.

"Keep it down! What's wrong with you?"

I told him what had just happened, still gasping, still in shock. Melissa chimed in, telling him that my attackers thought I was gay, probably thrown off by my size and that I was dancing with her.

When my comrade understood that the boys were Chicano, he'd heard enough. "Members of the underclass cannot be held responsible for their homophobia. It's in their culture," he said, practically spitting in rage. Just then the Communist Party member hosting the party came closer to inquire what was wrong. My comrade apologized, telling him that I had too much to drink and was being sent home.

I wanted to scream, to make him take back his wounding lies. He knew I rarely drank and never to excess, but I couldn't talk, my voice choked by too much pain. His treachery horrified me; I didn't know what I had done to deserve such condemnation. None of my friends came forward, although days later they told me they were in the back and didn't see me. By then it didn't matter. By then I would no longer be a member of the Revolutionary Union.

Melissa drove me to San Francisco General all the while railing against the organization that had just denied me. The ER doctor palpated my torso gently, making note of the heel-shaped bruises on my arms, legs, and abdomen. He sent me to x-ray and put the films up on the light box. Even I could see that four ribs were cracked through, the fractures displaced. There was a hairline fracture on my pubic bone. The doctor wanted to call the police, but I wouldn't let him. I just wanted to go home.

During the forty-five-minute ride back to San Jose, Melissa stirred up my anger and for the first time I saw myself as an anonymous cog in a machine that valued me no more than the corporate bosses valued their workers. The very people I depended on, comrades who I thought would do anything for me as I would do anything for them, just threw me away.

Confused and scared, I vacillated between anger at the RU and anger at myself for getting in so deep with them. Once home, my chest bound in a wide ace bandage, Melissa helped me comb through the past three and a half years until I could finally accept that the Revolutionary Union was not who they represented themselves to be. In fact, in their hierarchal and patriarchal structure, they were not so very different from the government and corporate model of top-down leadership they claimed to disavow.

Each breath pierced, exacerbating the pain of my ribs. I couldn't sleep, I was in too much pain and there was so much to think about, to try to understand. As soon as I thought he might be awake, I called Barry Greenberg to ask for a meeting.

His voice dripped ice. "I was about to call you. Come over right away."

Melissa drove me to Barry's apartment and waited in the car. His door was open and through the screen door I saw him on the floor playing a board game with his school-age daughter. He looked up and gruffly sent her to a back room.

No preamble, he jumped right in.

"Calling attention to yourself at the party last night was very bad, Jody, and it was especially egregious to bring a civilian who had the audacity to suggest calling the pigs!"

"Wait a minute! You weren't there. Look at what they did!" I lifted up my shirt to show him the bandage and the bruises. "These guys jumped me, they broke four ribs. How does this make me wrong? I did nothing to provoke them, I wasn't drunk, hadn't even had a drink. I get that I shouldn't have brought my friend, but that is such a little thing compared to what happened. My comrades betrayed me, Barry. Nobody came over, nobody gave me support!"

I still believed enough in him to expect compassion, to believe I could talk to him and he would listen.

We were sitting on the ragged couch in his living room. Morning light edged through the closed curtains. On the kitchen table was a box of sugary cereal, teeth-gouged orange peels, and a crumbled napkin.

Barry's eyes were impenetrable, more opaque than granite.

"You must partake in extensive self-criticism and your comrades will decide what's to be done."

"I was beat up! And accused of being drunk! They should be criticized. They owe me an apology!"

He shook his head, about to open his mouth when suddenly I was upright, so quickly that I swayed from the blood rushing to my head.

"I quit!" I yelled. "You can all go fuck yourselves!"

For a moment, Barry and I were both shocked. That wasn't my intent when I first arrived. I had hoped to talk to him and my roommates before making a definitive decision. He recovered himself first.

"I've had my doubts about you from the start. You're not cut out for this, Jody. You're too much of an intellectual—you don't have what it takes to be a good communist." His mouth was a sneer of disdain.

I heard my mother's voice listing my failures, that I'd never be good enough, never measure up to my sister. All my courage and self-assurance fell away. An old squeaky valve pried open. Shame quenched the righteous confidence and anger I thought I was armored in. Tears swelled up—they always betrayed me—and I didn't dare say anything that might invite more. I wanted him to see me leave unbowed. Walking out in the throes of so much emotion, I stumbled twice on the stairs. Before I reached the car, I stopped in the building's entrance to smoke a cigarette. The feelings percolated up before I could suppress them.

Barry's final words to me during our meeting tapped into the infinite depth of guilt first elicited in the office of Dr. Frank.

Shame.

I had failed.

Shame on me.

19

STRUGGLE

After taking Melissa to the airport, I returned home to find the student collective meeting in the apartment I shared with Meg and Pamela. We had moved to the one-bedroom flat divided from a larger house a year before after Buffy tore up the carpet at yet another place. The small living room was crowded, Buffy asleep in the center.

Conversation stopped when I opened the door; Barry had obviously already reached them. I looked at each person, hoping somebody would say something. That I wasn't wanted was made clear by their silence. I went into the bedroom, gathered a few pieces of clothing, then into the kitchen for Buffy's bowl and leash, and walked out, her following. At the last minute I tossed my house key onto a side table, hard enough that it bounced onto the floor. Nobody called out, nobody followed me. I can still feel the stinging hurt of sadness and rejection. It was the RU's ideology that drew me in, but it was the community that kept me going, and without them it would be a long while before I would find myself again.

I drove over to the apartment of a man from the Gay Liberation Front whom I had recently met and felt an instant connection. He greeted me warmly and held me while I sobbed. My legs felt cut out from under me. No longer fit for the world I'd lived in since leaving home, I wondered where I could find a life anywhere else.

Several days later I had to call the apartment to arrange to pick up the rest of my things. Both my roommates were there, prepared to do battle with me.

"You can't do this, Jody. Stop and think about it. Nothing's happened that can't be fixed," Meg said, her forehead wrinkled, her chin wavering. I hoped she wouldn't cry—that would set me off and I needed to stay strong.

I was throwing clothes into a box I'd picked up behind a grocery store that still had bits of lettuce stuck to it. "I didn't see anyone speak up for me during the meeting."

"Everybody was shocked. We talked about nothing else after you left. You're such a valuable part of our collective but you take things so personally," Pamela said. "You shouldn't be so sensitive, Jody—you know we love you." Her face was full of concern, but she struck the wrong note.

"You sound like my mother! I'm too sensitive, is that it? I've heard that all my life. I was beat up. My attackers thought I was gay. Our comrade accused me of being drunk. Does that make me disposable? And that makes it all right? It doesn't matter. Last night was only the last straw. I've been thinking about quitting for a while but just wasn't sure."

Hearing myself say that out loud, I knew it was true.

They pleaded with me to reconsider, to apologize to Barry, to reaffirm what the RU stood for.

"I'm sorry. Maybe Barry was right. I've tried, you know I have, but it's impossible for me not to treat people as individuals rather than anonymous members of the masses. I'm sorry, Pamela and Meg, I'll miss you guys more than you can know."

I had very little furniture or household goods, only a mattress and two boxes of books and four more of clothes and sundry items. I brought them all to the room I found available in a house belonging to a woman I met in the Women's Liberation group the year before. Maggie lived with her six-year-old daughter in a side-by-side duplex across the street from the San Jose Airport. The small bedroom was perfect for Buffy and me.

But it was difficult, so difficult. On the streets in San Jose, everywhere I went, people associated me with the Revolutionary Union. They wanted to know what was happening, when the next rally would be. I didn't want to tell them that I had no idea. I spoke to nobody about what had happened, not even my new roommate. I barely understood it myself. Four months past my twentieth birthday, I felt no more mature than I had as a teenager on the streets of Hollywood. It was as though time had been suspended and I was right back to where I started.

When I apprised my parents of my new address, they asked me to return home. Knowing I was no longer in college, they saw no sense in my remaining in San Jose. I did consider it but saw no future in returning to my childhood bedroom. Without the ballast of the RU, I could see myself too easily sucked back into the drug scene and my mother's infantilizing domination.

20

RECLAIMED

One month later, in April 1972, I found a job at Fairchild Semiconductor in Sunnyvale, in the area not yet known as Silicon Valley. The irony did not escape me that I would be working at a factory, not for the purpose of organizing, but to pay the rent.

I was placed on the morning shift, 6:45—3:15, and assigned to the fabrication assembly line. The process and product fascinated me. Starting with round silicon wafers the size of a silver dollar, the final result was a transistor micro-processing chip that amplified, controlled, and generated electrical signals. These chips would be in everything electronic, but in 1972, the public hadn't yet heard of them.

The set-up was a series of processing stations. One job completed, the containers holding wafers passed on to the next worker. My job at the acid station was to dip the wafers already imprinted with circuit wiring into a vat of hydrofluoric acid for their final cleansing before being placed in hot diffusion tubes that would bake out impurities. The stink emitted was rotten eggs and decaying vegetables; hard to imagine I would get used to it, but I did.

At first the delicacy of the work made me nervous—I could be such a klutz. There was a splashguard and I did wear gloves, but at first I dipped the tray at arm's length in case I dropped it and caused the acid to splash out on me. After the first few times, Beverly, the lead worker, pushed me to work faster. There was a certain amount of time allowed for the wafers to travel down the line and our bonuses, which the woman depended on, were based on time and output.

Just behind me were two open diffusion tubes heated to more than 1,000 degrees centigrade. On my very first day, a woman at that station baked a melted cheese sandwich in one of the tubes and was fired immediately. The foreman and supervisor both tore into her, and it broke my heart when she cried and worried how she'd be able to feed her children. That earned her no sympathy, and even I had to agree that it was pretty stupid of her to contaminate a sterile environment. Perhaps if I were still in the RU, I would have mounted a protest in her defense, but in this new world, anonymity was what I sought.

It was careful but mindless work, freeing my thoughts to rake over the years gone past. I was beginning to see what I had missed between my drugged last years of high school to what would now be my third year of college. I hadn't cared or even taken note of how out of step I was with the rest of my generation. Now back in the world, I saw that I would have to start over, that the experiences common to late adolescence were still ahead of me. I had to relearn how to meet people without evaluating their readiness for recruitment. Mostly I had to relearn who I was as an individual now that I was no longer in the collective nest.

Of the nine other women on the line, most, like Beverly, had been there for years. They were kind to me, inviting me to join them at the lunch table. I was usually pretty quiet, feeling shy with these working-class women who didn't go to college and whose main conversation was the latest episode of one television show or another I'd never heard of. I was so different from them, my sort of life foreign to their world, theirs foreign to mine. Most were old enough to be my mother. Some old enough to be my grandmother.

Jimmy, our supervisor, took great pleasure in being a rooster amongst his hens. Several inches shorter than me, probably in his forties, the ex-baseball player going to fat often walked the line telling nasty jokes even while chastising us if we slowed down to respond. When he laughed at himself, he often patted the butt of a woman nearby. The other women seemed to enjoy him; at least, they appeared to.

Seeing how ruffled I got, the worker next to me said, "He's just a rascal. Pay him no mind."

Jimmy took the production team out for pizza every Friday after work and kept inviting me to join them, but I made excuses rather than admit I had neither the energy nor the desire to hang out with them during off hours. He made a plea again several months into my employment and when again I declined, he looked at me with sudden comprehension.

"Of course, how stupid of me. You're Jewish, right? I can always tell—it's the hair and skin. Pizza's not kosher, right? Besides, it's the Sabbath, you can't eat Friday night to Saturday, right?" He laughed in an unkind way. "Just Christian babies?"

"That's right," I heard one of the women say. "That's what my minister says."

I had never been singled out so blatantly for being Jewish. How did he even know I was, just from my hair? My last name wasn't the usual giveaway. My father, to avoid the discrimination he experienced in the Navy during World War II, changed it from Friedman to Forrester before I was born. A self-avowed "orthodox atheist," he hated being identified as Jewish when he didn't think of himself that way.

Like so many Jewish kids, although unbelieving in the religion, I was always aware of the charged atmosphere that practically screamed that the other shoe must drop. It wasn't a question of "if" but "when." There were "us" and "them" and if a line were drawn, if Jews were again the targets of hate, most of my friends would be forced to one side and I forced to the other. It had happened that way in Europe, when all of a sudden Jews living comfortably for generations with their Christian neighbors were deserted, left to their own defenses, and ultimately horrific deaths. In my earliest years, I got the message that it could happen here.

I'd had minor slaps of anti-Semitism in the past, but this was a punch and brought on a rush of anger so intense that my hands clenched, ready to strike. Jimmy's eyes and mouth opened wide. He took a step backward, but just in time I remembered where I was and dropped my hands.

"You're such an asshole, Jimmy, that's not..." Whatever I was about to say got stuck in throat spasms cutting off my breath. I didn't want to get fired and could feel how close my temper was pushing me. Standing close to the exit, I pushed the door open and left the building in a run to avoid the storm that must have blown in a few hours earlier. I got in my car, started the engine, turned it off, and threw open the door to stomp back in through the front entrance and take the stairs two at a time to see my supervisor.

He startled when I yelled, while still outside his door, dripping rain. "I can't work for Jimmy anymore!" Dan, an avuncular middle-aged man, pointed to the chair in front of his desk and closed the door. He sat on another chair, offered me a cigarette, lighting them both before handing one to me.

"What's the problem?" he asked.

"Jimmy's impossible, he's a chauvinist pig and I've had enough!"

"What happened, Jody?"

But I couldn't tell him, gut-paranoid that he would add to Jimmy's insults or that he would tell me I was overreacting, too sensitive.

"I'd rather not tell you. Isn't there another team you can put me on?"

"This isn't the way we do things. You would have to go through personnel and file a complaint."

My head shook, my shoulders sprung tight. I couldn't deal, not at all. Getting up, thinking just to get away before I broke down, Dan held up a hand to stop me.

"But," he said, picking up a pink memo note from his desk, "I just got this. Edie in laser had to take an emergency leave of absence so I'll put you in there until we can resolve something more long-term. I'll meet you in the cafeteria in ten minutes and bring you over."

I held my sobs until I got to the women's bathroom where if anyone else were there, they would have been scared by my anguished breakdown. When I couldn't wait any longer, eyes red-rimmed and swollen, I cleaned my glasses and put my mouth under the cold water faucet to drink deeply.

Dan brought me to a small lab where a machine was set up to etch the wafers with a laser microscope. The work was detailed, requiring precision and concentration to set the parameters for each wafer to be divided into tiny analog semiconductor chips. I found that I enjoyed the exactitude of dialing in the measurements through the oversized laser microscope and watching the red light slicing each wafer, but what I best remember was the relief of being alone, away from Jimmy, away from the stink of rotten eggs.

After working at so many jobs where I chafed against supervisors I couldn't respect, what I would take away from this time on the line was how important it would be to someday work for myself. My temperament just wasn't suited to take orders. This knowledge set the stage for my pursuit of chiropractic medicine, a profession where I could be self-employed, where nobody could tell me what to do or how to do it.

21

EXPOSED

About to go for ice cream with my roommate's daughter and her two young friends, the phone rang. I knew it was my mother—I had a feeling for her calls.

"Jody, what's going on? What have you been doing?" Her voice sounded strained as though she was trying not to cry, but I couldn't imagine why or what about.

"Nothing, Mom. I just put Buffy's leash on to walk over to San Carlos Street to get some ice cream. What's wrong, did something happen?" I handed my roommate Buffy's leash. She was straining to join the girls on the front porch.

I heard my dad's voice commanding my mother to give him the phone. This never happened. Even when my father answered the telephone, he automatically handed the receiver to my mother.

His voice was calmer than hers, though I could still hear tension.

"Dad, what's going on?"

"The FBI was here. They just left, and well, quite frankly,

they scared us." It was impossible to imagine my big strong father intimidated, but indeed he was.

"What? Tell me what happened, Dad."

My mom grabbed the phone. "The chicken just came out of the oven, I was dressing the salad and the doorbell rang. I jumped—you know how loud it can be!"

"Please. Calm down, Mom. It was the FBI? What did they say? What did they want?" I wrapped the coiled telephone cord around my finger, trying to be patient when I wanted to scream.

"Here, honey, tell her." My mom handed the phone back to my dad.

"Two men wearing grey suits, they show ID, they ask to come in. I said no, just tell me what you want." He sneezed, just getting over a cold.

"Good, Dad, that's good. Then what?"

"They showed us a book, a government book, very official looking." His hand covered the voice box as he whispered, "Shirl, hand it to me."

"Okay, this is the title. *America's Maoists, a report by the Committee on Internal Security, from the second session of the ninety-second Congress of the House of Representatives.* Do you know anything about this? Your picture is here on page 140."

"My picture? What is it? What do they want?"

I had never told my parents the extent of my political involvement. They had no idea about the Revolutionary Union or that I was a Maoist, no idea I'd ever been arrested. None of it.

"They want you to go to D.C. to testify to a committee, like the House of Un-American Activities, I think. It sounds like the McCarthy hearings, but I don't know. One of the guys said you were no longer a communist but have valuable information that will help their investigation," my dad said. "You're a communist?"

My mother took the phone again. "I told them you would, that we would buy you an airline ticket."

"Mom, put Dad back on and don't take the phone from him again!" I was reeling, trying to imagine what this was like for my parents, how disturbed and frightened they must be.

"Dad, they want me to testify? Did they say why they didn't come to me?"

"I asked, but typical civil servants, they're only doing what they were told. They left us the book, but we haven't looked through it yet. Jody, is it true? Were you in this organization?"

The children came back in. They were impatient and reminded me in whispers that the market closed in ten minutes.

"Dad, yes, it is true but I'm not any longer, not for at least a year. I'm so sorry but I've got to go. I'll call you later. I need to see this book before I know what to do."

"We're worried for you, Jody. Be careful."

The kids were arguing. All of them wanted to be first to hold Buffy's leash and I had to negotiate. I left the house wondering what the hell happened.

Although I hadn't been in contact with my comrades since I left the RU, once I was home I tried calling my ex-roommates and Charles, but nobody picked up or called back after I left messages on their answering machines.

The next morning, a note from my supervisor Dan was clipped to my time card telling me to come see him immediately. An official looking book sat on the center of his desk. He motioned me to sit; he remained standing. Picking up the grey covered paperback, he opened to the page he had paper-clipped.

"Is that you?" He pointed at the tiny photograph, willing to give me the benefit of the doubt. I wished for him that I could say it wasn't, but of course it was.

He handed me the book. It was thick, covered in government-issued cardboard and printed on cheap grainy paper. I hadn't pictured it so authentic while talking to my parents. Next to my picture, taken I don't know when or where, was my birth date. A description followed: "According to the [informants'] testimony, Forrester was active in the women's liberation movement and was an effective crowd agitator. She was a member in the student collective of the Revolutionary Union in San Jose."

I saw that it was the result of a House investigation, via FBI moles, into the RU during my time there. I remembered them, the informants—Larry Goff, always the loudest advocate of violent overthrow, and his wife Betty, an at-home mother of three, who worked in the community collective. We had a friendly relationship and she called me occasionally to babysit their children. Didn't that indicate they trusted me? Why would they betray me?

Apparently it mattered not, although as a mother now, I can't conceive of leaving my daughters with somebody I thought dangerous.

Above my photo was a picture of Miles F., the eager-to-kill comrade from that night in my living room, the same one who brought a gun to the lettuce strike.

"You know it is. How did you get this?" My voice was strangled, almost to a whisper.

He adjusted his tie, sat down and stood up again, buttoned his jacket, and walked to the window, turning his back to me. "Two FBI investigators just left. They want you to testify…"

I interrupted. "I know what they want. They spoke to my parents, but I won't, I can't." I pressed my fists on my eyes to dam the tears, but there were too many of them. I hated how at the ready my tears always were.

"I told them I've seen no evidence of you organizing. Are you still in this group?"

I shook my head. "No, it's been about a year but..."

"But you won't cooperate?" His voice was gentle, sympathetic.

"It's hard to explain. They're still my friends." I didn't want to go into it, not with him.

"You know I have to let you go, right?" He looked back at me and I nodded, staring over his shoulder at the ever-present Lower Peninsula haze. "I don't want to, Jody. You've been a good worker, one of the best on the line. But we're moving toward requiring high-security clearance for all our employees, and, well, you'll never pass."

I stood up when he came close, arm outstretched to shake my hand, but I was already out the door, anxious to get to my car before my tears turned to screams.

I applied to two other semiconductor factories in the area and was told twice I was hired, only to get a phone call the next day reneging the offer. I asked at the second place why they changed their mind.

The personnel woman's voice quieted. "I'm sorry, but the FBI came in to speak to my boss about your background. I really am sorry. We're short of hands and need someone with your experience."

The agents called on my parents again to tell them to persist in putting pressure on me. That put my father's back up. He didn't like being told what to do any more than I did and phoned me that night in support of my refusal.

Ultimately I was defeated. Without a job, I couldn't stay in San Jose much longer.

Discussing my options, my roommate and I sat on kitchen chairs in the backyard we rarely watered and even more rarely mowed. Dandelions and yellow mustard had long taken over, but the iris bulbs that Maggie planted in October pushed out pale green stems reaching for the sun. We each had a glass of wine in one hand, a lit cigarette in the other.

"Where will you go?" she asked. Maggie was only eighteen when she met her husband-to-be at an Air Force base near her hometown of Dothan, Alabama. She left the Deep South and her family to follow him to California where she had to get used to a West Coast way of living previously unknown. I hoped to mimic her strength in the following months.

"I guess first to L.A., visit my folks, my friends, but I don't want to stay there. Maybe I'll see if I can crew a boat going to South America. Maybe I'll check out New York or Vermont." I kept shaking my head, my thoughts a skipping record stuck on the same scratch.

Maggie shivered. The chilly northeast held no appeal. Her daughter came out and I pulled her onto my lap. Fresh from a bath, she smelled like pineapples and coconut. I would miss her.

Maggie said one word. "Life."

"Right." I raised my glass to her.

"I've tried to picture you as a kid, but I can't. Were you always so loud, so rebellious?"

I laughed. "Always, I guess. In elementary school, I was the girl who talked too much, who couldn't stay in her seat, who talked back to the teachers. In junior high, I was the angry girl, choked with self-loathing and rebelling against the teachers I didn't respect. In high school, I hung with the pill poppers and pot smokers, few of whom made it through to graduation. I always fit in better with the outsiders, with others equally defiant of middle-class decorum and rules that made no sense."

Maggie, raised in a conservative home, laughed. "So you actually haven't changed all that much. I was such a good girl that it took me this long to realize that my family's expectations of me weren't my own. They wouldn't have known what to do with a child like you."

Her daughter's arms curled around my neck. "Don't go, Jody. You were going to take me to San Francisco to ride the cable cars, remember?"

I hugged her close. "Of course, I haven't forgotten. Let's go on Saturday. You know what else is happening on Saturday?"

She shook her head against my chest. This girl had become so precious to me, I wondered if she'd remember me.

"My twenty-first birthday."

"You're not as old as Mommy, but that's still pretty old!"

"Yep, that's for sure." I laughed. Maggie took her daughter in for a story and bed. I was cold, but the wine deadened my limbs and I didn't follow. I wasn't ready, not for any of this. Having once again lost the habit of making decisions for myself, I had no idea how to navigate. I was afraid to move on, but there was no longer anything for me in San Jose. I was finished there.

22

FREED

I spent the next six months in Los Angeles living with my parents, working at an insurance company to save money while trying to figure out where to go next. The FBI made one more attempt to reach me, but again ignored, they didn't call again. Toward the end of that hiatus, two friends on spring break from UCLA joined Buffy and me in my car for a road trip up the coast.

We landed in Vancouver, British Columbia, where on the third day I was seduced by Stanley Park. Crisscrossed with hiking trails, on a peninsula surrounded by water on three sides, it was the most beautiful place to be on that sunny day. The sky was cobalt blue, washed clean after days of rain. With Buffy sprawled nearby, I lay on my back on the grass under cherry trees whose blossoms were the color of bubble gum and felt roots stretching from my body anchoring me to the land. I felt at home as I'd never had before, alive with a sense of peace in the beauty. After that day, my friends returned to Los Angeles with Buffy and my car, although I did retrieve both dog and car once I decided to stay in Vancouver for what would be the next chapter in my life.

In Canada, my time in the RU was left behind without a whisper. I was still too confused by who I had been and too busy moving forward to think about the past.

I found a modern dance/improvisation studio to take the classes that I'd never had time for before. Gaining control of my body and learning the extent of my arms and legs made it possible for me to finally possess my size, to claim its length and breadth. I no longer felt small inside, no longer felt embarrassed looking down at men to meet their eyes.

In 1975, two years after leaving San Jose, I was driving in Vancouver city traffic and heard the announcement on the radio that the Vietnam War was over, victory claimed by the North Vietnamese. Although no longer active, my certainty in which side was right had not waned and I exulted at the power of my generation to influence an end to the war.

Except it wasn't long before reports filtered out that Ho Chi Minh, the poet and communist leader that I revered, sent his troops from the Vietnam Liberation League south along the shores of the southern Mekong Delta, burning down villages and killing women and children believed to have supported the South Vietnamese militias. My hero crashed from his pedestal, trampling my self-confidence regarding all things political. I had always thought that there were only good guys and bad guys, confirmed in the beloved Westerns of my youth, but now the good were acting so badly that I felt personally betrayed. I was angry with nobody more than myself.

It would be years before I would trust myself to take a stand on pretty much any issue. When political discussions came up, I felt inadequate to voice an opinion. All I could do was shrug my shoulders.

For most of the four years that I stayed in Vancouver, I worked at an afterschool recreation center in a housing project paid for by the province of British Columbia. When in 1976, the funding was not renewed, I decided to go into the Canadian bush to plant trees. Since moving there I had made several close friends who exemplified all that I admired. At home in their bodies and in nature, indifferent to the commercial world, they owned no more than could fit in a backpack or a van. Theirs was a vagabond life I admired, caravanning into Central America, spending a month in Oaxaca, maybe two in Guatemala, their leisure time paid for with spring and fall forays into the far northwest to replace trees in denuded forests.

When I apprised my parents of my plans, they urged me again to return to their home in Los Angeles.

"C'mon Jody, be real! You're not cut out to do hard labor, you won't have the endurance or strength," my father said. "Come on back to L.A. There's got to be a job here you're more suited to."

But I'd been on my own for too long and moving back in with my mother and father would be dangerous to the independence I'd gained in the seven years away from their home. Knowing that I could count on their safety net always threatened to make false my credentials as a mature adult. I still had something to prove, both to them and myself. Instead, I sent Buffy to them with a person I knew who was driving to Southern California.

With my friends' help, I found a foreman willing to take me on. He gave me two days to get myself to Prince George, an industrial city in north-central British Columbia. All I knew about my destination was that it had once been a trading post and was mostly pulp mills that depended on deforestation for their trees. That's where the planters came in, to reforest for future cuts. Abound with fantasies of exotic travel, I'd boarded a Greyhound outside the downtown station one dark spring morning at four-thirty. It wasn't until I saw my pristine backpack and new tent settled on top of worn suitcases and duffel bags that I began to feel uneasy. Warned that stores would not be nearby, the bus's luggage compartment held all that would clothe and comfort me for the four-month commitment ahead.

A muted palette of colors heralded the April dawn as the bus lumbered over a narrow river bloated with rainwater and ice-melt. The roadside, lush with yellow buttercup, golden paintbrush, and primrose fireweed of early spring already transformed the ubiquity of winter brown to a spectrum of color. In the distance I saw the river traverse hilly terrain toward distant mountains still snow-capped with winter. But the beauty did little to ease my mind. A lump in my stomach pushed against my diaphragm, making it hard to take a deep breath. I wondered if my father was right, if I was really up to living out of a tent in the bush, let alone working long days outside. It only then occurred to me that the friends I emulated were Canadian men, so different from me, an American, urban-bred female. Was I again trying to imitate men, to be accepted as one of the guys? Hoping I wouldn't embarrass myself, I both welcomed and dreaded the challenges that lay ahead.

After twelve long hours and five hundred miles later, the bus stopped at a weathered tin signpost riddled with bullet holes. Prince George, population 18,901. There was no depot, only a weather-silvered bench and a sign on an equally wind-worn pole saying that the bus south was due at 11:10 p.m. The few who got off with me were swept away in waiting cars. On the long stretch of highway, there were neither shops nor restaurants nearby. Dirt rustled up by a blustering wind rendered distant buildings ghostly. A steady stream of cars and trucks passed, bowling clouds of tumbleweed in their wake. On my watch I saw that it was 4:15. I was so far north that the sun was still high in the sky.

The foreman named Rick had only given me directions on which bus to be on, nothing more. I didn't have his telephone number or even know his last name, but it didn't matter—the only pay phone lay crushed on the ground, zigzagged by dozens of black tread marks. A half-hour passed, then another, and another. I baked in the heat haloed by undulating eddies of dust and dirt. I thought that I must be on the outskirts and wondered, if he didn't come, how long it might take me to walk into town.

Leaning against the pole by the road, I longed for the bed always there for me in my parents' home and the comfort foods always in their pantry and freezer. I knew they would welcome me, but as a born-again Canadian I was determined to show myself resourceful and capable. But there I was—alone—nobody to greet me, no stationmaster that I could ask for help.

I smoked, lighting one cigarette off another, butt to butt. I was hungry but had already eaten the little food I packed. A film of dirt cloaked the backpack that I bought only the day before, along with the lime-green tent and blue goose down sleeping bag. Sinking to the ground, sinking into self-pity, I felt desolate and abandoned, a feeling too familiar from my angsty adolescence. A mangy, skinny mutt came by sniffing for food. I hoped that he'd keep me company, but off he ambled, not looking back.

I renewed my resolve to take care of myself, no matter if I had to stick out my thumb and head back south, even though I had nowhere to go, having sublet my basement flat for the summer. My closest friends had all left Vancouver, tucked away in their own tree-planting camps. I had hoped to work alongside them but their crews were already full.

At last, more than three hours later, the dusk still held off by the waning sun, a much pocked and dented pick-up truck pulled up alongside me. The blonde, bearded driver neither introduced himself nor asked me my name. Remaining in the cab, the engine still running, he indicated with a chin point that I was to climb in the back among boxes of groceries and coils of ropes. I expected more—something like how nice to meet you, sorry I'm late, how're you doing, where're you from—but apparently I was only a name on his to-do list he could now tick off.

We soon reached his house where I met the rest of the crew. To my relief, they were all very welcoming. In the group of eleven there were two other girls, their advantages immediately noted—both were with boyfriends and both seasoned planters. Everybody greeted me as a friend, happy to have somebody new amid mostly the same group that had planted the last few seasons together. That night we slept in our sleeping bags spread out on the living room floor. Full of nerves, I slept little until the morning arrived with the welcome smells of bacon and coffee made by Rick's wife Andrea.

A four-hour drive in a boxy panel truck called a crummy took us further northeast into the bush, the last two on one after another dry and furrowed dirt road. Andrea and Rick sat up front while the crew bounced on parallel benches in the cargo space. A joint passed around. Two of the boys played Beatles songs on old, scratched-up guitars. Most of them came from small towns throughout Canada and were fascinated that I had grown up in Los Angeles, a city they likened either to Gomorrah or an iconic Hollywood production.

We finally stopped in an alpine meadow, carpeted with rainbows of wildflowers, nestled in the foothills of the snow-topped Rocky Mountains. With years of practice, Rick organized us into teams to set up a kitchen tent, an outhouse, and a sauna. A large canvas tent was erected for sleeping, which I hadn't known would be there when I brought along my two-man backpacking tent. Nevertheless, I would be glad to have the bit of privacy it would afford.

The oversized waxed cartons that held the pine seedlings we would plant were emptied and flattened to construct the walls of a sauna next to a fast-moving creek. Once erected, the structure was enveloped in thick sheets of plastic. The men installed a wood-burning stove called an airtight in a circle of boulders that I helped fish out from the Arctic water.

I shivered. "It's cold!"

"Really? I hadn't noticed." Rick's lip curled.

This was the first time he spoke directly to me. I looked away but could feel his scowl at my back. He seemed to take an instant dislike to me; it would be awhile before I found out why.

That first night, after a dinner of roasted chicken and stuffed peppers cooked on the propane stove by Andrea, a fire was made and a bottle of Southern Comfort and a few joints passed around. It felt so like camping with friends that I had no thought of the next day when I crawled into my tent and wriggled inside my down bag for the night. The whiskey and pot high rode into my dreams and I was sure that I had just shut my eyes when the morning bell rang.

Nervous about the day ahead, I found my way to the kitchen tent to grab a few spoonfuls of granola and a mug of coffee before Rick shepherded us into the crummy to drive out to the logged slopes. The rising sun opposite the waning crescent moon was just beginning to allay the night's inky blackness. My first deep breaths made me lightheaded and giddy. I laughed as I climbed into the truck and my fellow planters laughed at me, the city girl in the bush for the first time, wearing a flannel shirt not yet faded and Dickey work jeans still creased from the shop shelves.

The hills that we were to plant were in sharp contrast to the nature that housed us. A pervasive smell of wood fire, not like a campfire but more like a house burning, wrapped us like cloaks. Slick with morning dew and strewn with charred slash left behind by the loggers who preceded us, the scorched slopes were nothing like the forests they had once been. Instead they presented as a surreal vision of Dante's seventh circle of Hell. It made me ache to look at them.

Rick dropped each experienced planter off at a pre-designated start place then jumped out with me. He clipped a sack of pine seedlings around my waist. It weighed too much to straighten up, though I soon found out that hardly mattered—it would be easier to plant staying close to the ground.

In the slash, there were no furrows, no guides to measure off. Rick was exacting as he stressed that it was most critical to stay on an imagined line, the goal a red flag half a kilometer away. He showed me how to stomp on a narrow shovel to make a slit in the ground, how with the shovel wedged in to insert the tree with roots untangled, then close the v-shaped cut with a thump of a heel. Shovel, wedge, plant, thump, count off ten steps. Do it again.

"Okay, you head toward the red flag, then the next one and the next one. Got it?" he asked, already turning away.

"Sure," I said, not sure at all, but hoping I would be able to translate his instructions to the actual job once he left.

Once I was alone, I obsessed over each seedling, trying to tease out the bunch of hair-like roots with my fingers until I realized that my fastidiousness was unfounded, that it only took one hard shake to free them. Speed was what counted. We were paid by the tree, about twenty cents each, counted not by what we had emptied from our sack but for the trees Rick would later ascertain had been planted well. An experienced planter might earn close to $200 a day. The other people were distant blobs of color and though far away I could see that they were going at twice my pace. I planted maybe a hundred in the six hours before Rick collected us and during that time I hadn't stopped moving, eyes on the ground, counting off steps, feeling his breath on my neck. He was not impressed when he saw how many trees were still in my bag. It was the other planters who reassured me with stories of their own early days.

That night there was no campfire, no weed, no drinking. A thick silence settled over the camp by eight o'clock even though the sun still hovered high above the mountains. I crawled into my sleeping bag and didn't realize that I had fallen asleep until the breakfast bell awakened me the next morning. Dangling drops clustered along the top tent seam fell on my face. I had a can of Snow Seal in my backpack, still unopened. A more experienced camper would have known to waterproof the tent the night before. I unzipped the door and was further alarmed to see snow powdering the ground. Steve, the only other novice planter there, caught my eye while I sat cross-legged in the door of my tent, reluctant to leave my sleeping bag's downy warmth.

"Can I bring you a cup of coffee?" he asked. His face was round with brown eyes and lashes that were more deer-like than human. I had already noticed him, and his attention in that moment warmed me.

But there was no time—there wasn't enough snow to deter the planting. I had less than ten minutes to dress myself, eat, make a lunch, and pile in the crummy, shovel and two bags of trees on my lap.

For much of the first week, I felt like I had the flu. Every bone, muscle, and tendon ached, more than I had known possible. My hips were bruised from the tree bags banging on them. Chapped lips, torn fingernails, dirt embedded in every crease. I got used to putting on clothes still crusted with grime from the day before and the day before that. The mornings were the hardest, but the end of the day not much easier. The sauna helped and I stretched and that helped too, but still I walked like a cowboy used to life in a saddle.

I envied the girls, Gillian and Susan, shorter than me by more than seven inches. My back ached from the bending; the ground was so much closer to them than me. But I was surprised to find that they envied my man-sized hands. For planting they were an asset, as well as my long legs that could stride up a hill, one step to their two. As each day I planted more trees and made better time, the labor showed me what I was capable of and it was no small joy. In the bush, my big-boned strength served me well, and the discovery that I could fall asleep and pass the night free of my usual restless dreams and nightmares seemed miraculous.

Rick never did warm up to me. He told Steve that had he known I was an American he never would have hired me. One evening we gathered in the kitchen tent for a meeting. Seriously fatigued, I tripped over a loose shoelace walking in.

"Don't they teach you how to walk down there?" Rick said.

People laughed—I blushed.

"He's just that way," Gillian said later. "Don't take it personally." But how could I not? I felt intensely the echoes of my foreman, Jimmy, at the semiconductor factory.

Steve continued to pay special attention to me and I to him. He poured my morning coffee and put milk in my cereal while I battled the thick sleep that always took a while to shake off. We rubbed the knots out of each other's necks and shoulders that by the end of the day no longer felt human. A new romance while working in the bush was unlike any other. We played out our courtship with a small but attentive audience who were excited by our coupling for the change in routine it provided.

Steve was a few years older, twenty-nine to my twenty-four, and worked in construction as a finish carpenter. He had already made himself indispensable at camp—there was nothing he couldn't jerry-rig, a much-valued skill when far from civilization. He was also several inches shorter than me. In the past that would have been enough to dissuade me, but my attraction to him overrode my vanity. Especially when I felt how well we fit when horizontal. As my body transformed to lean, brown, and strong, it was no longer the nemesis I'd always felt it to be. On the hills I was becoming more and more at home in my skin and the urban stereotype of tall man, short woman wasn't a good enough reason to deny what was happening between us.

At the end of most days I experienced an electrical-like rush of triumph that ameliorated the constant pain and fatigue. I hadn't known that I would be happier on my feet, working outdoors, than I had ever been in an office or factory where I was chronically short-tempered and easily frustrated. In the bush there were no office politics, just bodies working hard and sweat translating into currency. The hard walk, mountain air, and the peace of the bush so far away from city noise and distractions suited me well.

I still have a black and white photograph that Steve took of me in the low light of morning. I'm wearing a hooded sweatshirt, dirty work pants with multiple loops meant to hold tools, running a brush through my hair. I look happy. I was happy. I was in love.

We spent the evenings cuddled in my tent making plans to find an apartment in Vancouver for the summer before returning to the slopes for fall planting. Then we would travel, maybe to South America, maybe to Europe. Our promises to each other heartened me; there was a future, something to look forward to. I thought him an unexpected wonder. I didn't know then that once back in the city among our own friends and commitments, our relationship would be sorely challenged, and a year later run itself out.

We completed the first job in the designated four weeks and shut it down. The next camp could only be accessed by helicopter. We were flown in four at a time, squeezed in among boxes of supplies and trees. The slopes there were even steeper, the debris left by the loggers thicker and more slippery from recent rains. Our shovels had to be switched for mattocks, a tool much like a long-handled ax, but with a broad end instead of narrow. Only a mattock could penetrate the deeper slash.

This time one of the other planters rather than Rick showed me how to swing the nine-pound mattock over my shoulder, aiming for just the right spot to make the v-cut, then place the seedling and bring the mattock down again to close the hole. It was only efficient if done in two smooth moves and for the first few days I was back to planting less than a hundred trees a day. When my arms and shoulders begged me to stop, I refused, counting on my thinning pride to fuel the impetus necessary to keep going. I would not give in to my parents or Rick, both of whom expected me to fail.

In this more demanding environment, there were battering thunderstorms, vicious black flies, even more vicious midges. But there were also the Northern Lights revealed in diaphanous layers of ruby red, topaz gold, and sapphire blue spread out over the burnt mountain ranges in a soupy mixture. The Milky Way's cascade of white spiral fingers swam alongside rainbows of rich color. If the multitude of starry lights had burst into an operatic aria, I would not have been surprised. It remains to this day on the short list of spectacular events that I've witnessed.

Several times we were surprised by storms that sent us scurrying back to camp. Backgammon, cribbage boards, and cards came out then. The rain pelting the plastic made explosive snaps not unlike gunshots, and the swamp-like heat suffocated. Clouds of black flies and midges prowled, their bites raising itchy welts on my exposed neck and hands that were near impossible not to scratch. I still have scars.

Stories of childhood came up and I volunteered some of my own, harmless things like roller-skating competitions on our block and cards clipped on bicycle wheels.

Gillian's question surprised me. "What are you, Italian?"

"What?" I was confused about what she was asking me.

"It's just that you don't look American."

"What does an American look like?" Steve asked. He was sitting on the floor between my knees while I pressed my elbow into his tight shoulders. "Harder, Jo, yes, right there!"

"You know. White skin, straight hair."

"My family's from Eastern Europe, mostly Russia."

"Are you Jewish?" Drew asked.

"Yep," I said, not wanting to say more. I wasn't about to explain to them that yes, I was Jewish, but on a cellular level, more identifying with the heritage and culture than observant of the religion.

Rick stood up and walked out, but not without shooting me a look meant to wither. Worse than being an American, I was also a Jew. Having already had that experience at the factory, I was highly sensitized to anti-Semitism. My face heated.

"I've never known anyone Jewish," Gillian said. "My pastor said Jews had horns, but he was pretty crazy."

"Jesus, Gillian, get real," Steve said. When my hands fisted on his neck, he stood up.

"My grandmother's nose was hooked and she claimed that the worst thing that ever happened to her, like ever, was being taken for a Jew after spending a summer in the sun," Susan said.

"Good thing she wasn't. Then she would have had far worse things to worry about."

My voice was harsh, maybe too harsh, but I didn't care. Steve pulled me outside while I worked to rein myself in. The camp environment was a casual one, not a place for arguments or debate. I wasn't so much angry as unbelieving that anybody would consider being thought a Jew the worst thing that could happen to them.

I continued to appreciate my body's strength and agility, when three and a half more weeks in, a pile of slash covering a deep stump hole tripped me up. My left foot sank in toe-first, wrenching my ankle as I fell backward with all my weight as well as the weight of the tree bag. The pain was so acute that I knew right away it was bad. I looked around frantically but saw nobody in shouting range. I wanted to scream, to rage, at the barren mountains, and most especially at Rick, but already knew the futility of it. More than a mile from camp, I was on my own and would have to get myself, by myself, off the mountain and back to our settlement. Rescue would not be forthcoming.

I sat up on the edge of the knee-deep hole, whimpering as I lifted each branch to unsnarl the thick roots that trapped my heavy leather and spiked cork boots, wishing only to roll time back a few minutes to avoid what had just happened. Extricating my foot was no small doing and it was a few minutes before I dared try to stand. The ankle crumbled when I put weight on it, making me fall down again, hard enough to bruise my tailbone. When finally I was able to talk myself into again trying to get up, I kept testing the foot to prove to myself that I actually was injured and not just babying myself. My mother always thought I was faking when I said I had a bellyache or headache, and I had internalized her doubt in my body's honesty, but the foot could really not bear weight.

I considered leaving behind the trees and mattock, but I knew that to Rick they were more valuable than me. Butt-scooting down the hill, using the ax as a crutch, I made it to the logging road, sweat dripping into my eyes. I sat dazed, awash again in self-pity, feeling a knife stabbing my ankle that twisted and jabbed. As I limped down the road taking frequent rests, more than anything I dreaded seeing Rick. My default guilt at failing to please added to the weight of shame for my lack of forbearance, exactly as my father had predicted. I practiced smiling, even tried a few chuckles in preparation for my arrival at camp. I could not bear for anyone to see how fragile I was. One abiding principle in my life was never to reveal weakness.

To my great relief, the camp was deserted and I made it unnoticed to my tent. Several hours later, in Steve's embrace, I could finally cry. He cut off my boot revealing a puffy ankle swelled to twice its size.

As expected, Rick was pissed.

"You're going to cost me. As if my workers compensation isn't high enough. I should have known better than to hire a Yankee!"

He stood there a moment, his frown a rictus of contempt. As though I wanted to be disabled, as though I wanted to be sent home. Worse, I was stranded—the helicopter wouldn't arrive for several more days.

Steve carved a branch for a cane so I could hop on my good foot. I assisted Andrea in the kitchen where I could sit while slicing and mixing or spoon out raw dough onto a cookie pan. I washed dishes until my fingers, no longer cracked and dusty, pickled in the water.

By the time the helicopter came in carrying supplies, Rick was overtly hostile, asserting that I was exaggerating my injury. The entire crew protested his treatment of me, but he could not be dissuaded from his belief that Americans, let alone Jews, were not to be trusted. I was not at all happy to hear that Rick would also be on the helicopter back to Prince George.

When the time came to go, the crew crowded around with hugs and kisses. I wiggled my way into the jump seat behind Rick, stuffed between five bags of trash to be dumped in town. A piece of paper in my pocket with the address of one of Steve's close friends in Vancouver made it easier to leave him. He was pretty sure I could stay with her until he returned.

That was that—my adventure was over.

From the helicopter I had a wide-angle view of where we'd been. A forest of old growth trees surrounded acres of stripped swaths of charred debris. That the pine trees I planted would eventually be absorbed into that tableau struck me with awe at nature's ability to survive.

The back door next to my seat shuddered when we first lifted off. Like a window rattled by wind or a trash truck driving down the street.

"The door's locked, right?" I asked the pilot.

He nodded but didn't look back, concentrating instead on getting the helicopter above the tree line. Rick shot me a dirty look. I shut up, but I couldn't ignore feeling threatened by the continued rattling of the door. Typical of my deference to men in charge, I didn't question the pilot again, but I wished I had when we reached Prince George fifteen minutes later.

As the helicopter hovered twenty feet above the landing pad, the door flew open. It happened in a second, so quickly that had I not felt the pull of gravity and the wind blasting in, I still might not believe that it actually happened. There was nothing solid to grab onto; I began to slide. I don't remember if I screamed, but likely I did. It seemed like the last possible minute before the pilot tipped the helicopter, allowing me to fall away from the flapping open door onto the garbage bags.

Once we were on the ground the pilot, his face bloodless, mouth slack, and eyes wide open, ran to the open door.

"Are you okay? Jesus Christ. That's never happened before!" His Adam's apple slid up and down as though seeking a way out. "Are you okay?" he asked again. He helped me slide down to the tarmac, but I collapsed to my knees, forgetting my leg could no longer support me.

Rick said "Typical!" and turned to walk away, dismissing me with a frown and narrowed eyes.

"You're an asshole, Rick. A fucking asshole!" There was so much more I wanted to say but those were all the words I could get out. I knew that even had I found the right words, he would take no notice. He kept walking toward the offices, shaking his head.

"Can I do anything for you?" the pilot asked. I shook my head, only wanting to be left alone.

I limped to the terminal and to the shuttle that would take me back to the desolate post that I had first arrived at. It wasn't too long a wait for the southbound coach. The pristine backpack, tent, and boots that had been stored in the baggage compartment on the bus north were now a uniform dirt-grey, embedded with mud. This time I knew where I was traveling to. One consolation was that I would see my good friends soon, whose stories of camp life I could now contribute to.

The drive south was a different ride altogether than my anxious trip north only six weeks before. In the bush I was what I thought of as the best version of myself. I planted more than two thousand trees with my size twelve feet, man-sized hands, and thick-boned long legs. Sitting with my foot outstretched, waves of an unfamiliar feeling coursed through my thoughts—a prideful sense of satisfaction. Despite my self-doubts, despite my parents' concerns, despite Rick's hostility, I did what I set out to do. This body that had always felt alien was now a friend, the person I was on the inside finally matching up with the person I appeared to be outside, uniting both with a warm sense of completion.

The riot of wildflowers blooming on the trip north now spilled onto the road, the river we crossed now swift running. The snow clinging to the mountaintops above the tree line was mostly melted, leaving white thin streaks like cake frosting drips in their wake.

Now, from the distance of more than forty years, I pictured the trees I planted sturdy and robust, their branches laden with cones. Like me now, rooted with my family, my branches extending through the DNA of my daughters.

EPILOGUE

Breaking from the Revolutionary Union was the hardest and most traumatic thing I had ever done. Without the stability of the collective, I became lost in a world that had gone on without me. No longer at ease with people, I didn't know how to relax or hang out without purpose. The vocabulary of the revolution inscribed on my tongue made normal conversation the greatest challenge of all.

Thinking it better to bury the memories in a tomb of silence, I resolved early on to tell nobody about my time as a revolutionary. I didn't want the new people in my life to judge me, for them to see me as a foolish risk-taker. I felt too much shame about my stupidity and bad judgment, but even more punishing, too much guilt about my failure to be a good communist.

I also maintained secrecy because the RU's position on security and covertness was deeply ingrained. Even writing this book felt too much like I was betraying my comrades, like I was pulling curtains away from a room meant to be kept dark forever. Imagining what they might say, I felt tremulous, unsure if I got it right. But what's "it"? And what's "right"?

I'd kept my participation in the Revolutionary Union a secret from everyone I'd met, the only exception being my husband. To no one did I care to reveal that I once sat in my living room with a M1 aimed at the door anticipating a visit by the cops I called pigs.

It wasn't until I began writing this book that I told my children and friends about those years of my life. Initially I couldn't meet their eyes, staring at my knees instead—I was so embarrassed. But nobody responded as I thought they would. Not, how could you have been so stupid and so violent? Instead they expressed admiration for my dedication, understanding it as a viable response to the consciousness and passion of the sixties rather than violent impulses or shortcomings of my own. Their positive response loosed me from decades of needless mortification, finally freeing me to embrace the spirit, courage, and heart of the daring young woman I was.

I returned to Los Angeles after a season of travel with Steve. Twenty-six years old, I was ready to pursue the education that would lead me to become a chiropractor, a profession where my size proved to be an asset.

My children and husband tell me so often that they love me that I have no choice but to believe I must be loveable. Over time my parents and I reconciled in a deeper way.

One night in 1990, they were at our house for dinner. My father sat on the couch watching my husband and me juggle our newborn and toddler. Tears trailed down the deep crevices on his cheeks.

Never had I seen my strong father cry. I couldn't even imagine it. Alarmed, I asked him what was wrong.

"I wish you and John had been my parents. Then I could have been the father to you that you deserve. I'm sorry, Jody." He died only a few months later, too early, at age seventy-seven.

Thirteen years later, my mother called me from her nursing home on a Sunday morning.

Her voice garbled by the aggressive Parkinson's disease invading her body, she said, "I love you, Jody. I love you."

Never had she said those three words to me—never did I expect to hear them. A nurse phoned me only hours later to tell me she had passed.

I'll always be grateful for those end-of-life gifts from my mother and father. They were a welcome balm that went far to soften long-felt hurts.

All the evidence of my years in the Revolutionary Union lay now in crooked stacks on the floor in my office. After nearly eight years of writing and revising, the time came to put away the piles retrieved from the box that for years I'd kept in various garages along the way. I considered what to keep and what to toss and in the end decided to keep it all. If nothing else, I housed a unique and remarkable archive of that historically tumultuous era.

The original brown box was too wilted and crumpled to be of further use. Spider legs and fly wings tangled in clumps of dog hair, dirt clods dusted the bottom. Before I cut the box down for recycling, I shook it out in the alley behind our house, launching the debris to the ocean breeze.

ACKNOWLEDGMENTS

Deepest gratitude to my publisher, Michelle Lovi, of Odyssey Books, for her belief in and enthusiasm for my story.

So many people to thank—family, friends, teachers, mentors. First, Askold Melnycyzk, instructor at the Bennington Writing Seminars, who sowed the seeds of this book in 2008 when he asked me what my story was, and I realized this was it.

Writer and instructor Samantha Dunn, of the Writers Workshop in Los Angeles, further fertilized them. Her early encouragement and edits helped me see that I actually had a book, something I never thought possible.

Suzanne Sherman, writer and memoir coach, offered further edits and support.

Emily Rapp Black, of Blueprint Manuscript Consulting, stuck by me to the end and helped bring it home.

I am particularly grateful to Deborah Weiss, my oldest friend, whose intuitive reading guided me when I was floundering.

Further thanks to fellow writers, Ginger Eager and Lili Flanders, for their unconditional belief in my worth as a storyteller.

A resounding thank you to my parents, Bob and Shirley Forrester, who generously gave me the portable typewriter that I requested for my tenth birthday so "you could write your stories."

And especially, my deepest appreciation to my husband, John Schneider, and to my daughters, Emily and Erin Schneider. I don't know how many times they read one part or another of this book, but they always said yes when I asked and always told me the truth when I needed it. Their unconditional love and belief in me as a writer sustains me daily.

ABOUT THE AUTHOR

Jody A. Forrester was born and raised in Los Angeles during the uneasy Fifties and tumultuous Sixties. She graduated from high school in 1969, while the Vietnam War was raging and the country increasingly divided along racial and class lines. When a freshman at San Jose State University, she joined a communist organization advocating armed overthrow of the United States government. In this memoir, Jody reaches into her past to understand how she came to embrace such a violent culture.

A chiropractor by profession, she was forced into retirement by a hand injury requiring surgery. With her time suddenly open, Jody was able to return to her first love, writing fiction and nonfiction stories. She pursued a BA in literature and writing at Antioch College/Los Angeles (2007), and a MFA, also in literature and writing, at Bennington Writing Seminars (2010).

Jody's essays and short stories have appeared in the *Sonora Review, Two Hawks Quarterly, WriteRoom, Dreamers Writing, Citroen Review, Gazelle* and several others. A story received an honorable mention in the Anderbo/Open City Competition (2009) and another story was featured in the 6th Annual Emerging Voices Group Show (2010) in Los Angeles.

She lives in Venice, California, with her husband, John Schneider, in the house by the beach where they raised their two daughters, Emily and Erin.

www.jodyaforrester.com

BOOK CLUB DISCUSSION

1. In terms of the political and cultural upheavals in the 1960s and 1970s, what was happening in your own life? Did the story show you a new side to any events that you were already familiar with?
2. What are the two or three most important themes or big ideas that run through the book? How successful is the author in intermingling her personal and political stories?
3. Within the first chapter when the author describes the almost shoot-out with the police, what feelings did that bring up for you? Did it make sense to begin the story with that incident before going into the backstory?
4. What about the author's life most resonates with you? Did you find anything particularly inspiring?
5. Discuss the narrator's transition from love as the answer to racism and economic disparity to a communist ideology. Given the times, does that make sense, not personally for you, but for her?
6. Do you see parallels between the political environment then and now?
7. Share a favorite passage from the book. Why did this section stand out?
8. What incidents, events, or moments did you find particularly moving and why? How did you feel when you finished the book? What were the take-aways for you?

9. What struck you most about the author and her life's journey?
10. If you got the chance to ask this author one question, what would it be?

www.ingramcontent.com/pod-product-compliance
Lightning Source LLC
Chambersburg PA
CBHW021435080526
44588CB00009B/535